THE POLITICS OF APE AND MACHINE

Power as Organization

JOSEPH COSTELLO

N/A
BOOKS
nabooks.org

CONTENTS

"The most difficult political problem facing mankind is the centralization of power in highly technological societies."

— LAWRENCE GOODWYN, *DEMOCRATIC PROMISE,*
1976

"There will be a further increase of useful things for useless people."

— IVAN ILLICH, *TOOLS FOR CONVIVIALITY,* 1970

"It is quite conceivable that the modern age—which began with such an unprecedented and promising outburst of human activity—may end in the deadliest, most sterile passivity history has ever known."

— HANNAH ARENDT, *THE HUMAN CONDITION,* 1956

INTRODUCTION

These are a series of essays written over three years on the politics of technology and the desperate need for basic reform of the systems of modern republicanism. No technology is politically neutral. Any technology adopted by a society reshapes that society, this social reshaping is politics. How any technology is structured shapes the politics built around, atop, and through it. For some technologies, this shaping can be relatively insignificant; for others this shaping is defining.

The book is fashioned around the first and main essay, "The Politics of Ape and Machine: Power as Organization." Subsequent essays further expand the ideas of the first essay. Certain themes, ideas, and examples used in the first essay will be repeated and expanded upon in the essays that follow. It is important to understand this is not a traditional narrative, but much more a mosaic. Each essay can be read alone, and together they create a larger portrait, a portrait necessary to step back from and bring in some of your own thoughts to fully conceive. It seeks to be an initial portrait of politics for the 21st century.

The great MIT mathematician and computer scientist Norbert Wiener, who is responsible for the basic concept and equations of feedback prevalent in all today's automated systems, stated America was a "know-how" society, but technological development demanded we become a "know-what" society. This understanding is fundamental for any politics of technology. All technological development is a choice, there is nothing deterministic about its adoption, yet, once any given technology is adopted, the technology plays a role, great or small, determining the future.

"Know-what" demands an encompassing understanding of humanity, not just the "know-how" of the development and operation of a given technology. The development of technology must be removed from the exclusive control of experientially narrow and imaginatively constrained technologists. The politics of any technology only starts with its development and initial implementation. It is then necessary to incorporate its societal and environmental impacts through feedback. This requires a healthy politics.

From stone tools to the harnessing of fire, *Homo sapiens* have been shaped by technology for literally millions of years. In the last two centuries, with the birth of industrialism, in a literal blink of an eye we have completely reshaped society and the planet itself. We are at the dawn of a new technological era, yet we have not seriously addressed the societal restructuring and environmental impact of industrialism. We are in great need of a politics of technology. This book hopes to offer a beginning.

THE POLITICS OF APE AND MACHINE

Homo sapiens evolved as social animals. From our beginnings, people lived and survived collectively as organized units, whether family, tribe, community, city-state, nation, empire or a combination of all. The identity of every human individual who ever lived was defined through the social organization they were part. With social organization, power is defined. Without social organization, any individual, whether Pharaoh or CEO, is simply an individual. Only by understanding social organization in all its configurations – political, economic, cultural, and technological – do we derive any ability to understand power. The understanding of power as organization is the most fundamental politics.

In today's politics, the concepts, structures, and processes of social organization are largely absent. There are numerous reasons for this void of organizational understanding. Most importantly, established power always seeks to obscure or outright prohibit thinking about the organization that upholds their power. All power requires acceptance of the organization it is based on, either through voluntary acquiescence or force. Discussion of alternative structures and processes is basically *haram*. Accepted politics in any given power structure always falls short of challenging the organization of power itself.

Much political history and understanding could be helpfully rewritten with a profoundly simple look at the actual structural organization of power, whether it's political, cultural, or economic. With the still relevant categories of the Ancient Greeks, the organization of power conforms to geometric patterns. Centralized, hierarchical power — oligarchy, monarchy, and tyranny — all take the shape of a pyramid. Power is concentrated with a few at the top, vertically spreading down to a powerless mass base. Decision making and the ability to act, *power*, is concentrated at the top.

Democracy is more unwieldy, horizontally organized. Power is distributed. Decision making and resulting action partially resides with each individual member of an organization, but the greatest power resides with the decisions and actions taken collectively. Democracy cannot be conducted through centrally organized power, nor can tyranny be afflicted through distributed power.

Across recorded history, centralized hierarchical order has overwhelmingly been the rule, distributed democratic order the exception. Hierarchical centralized organization is humanity's accepted traditional norm. Historically, discussion of any alternative or even the ability to conceive of alternatives largely absent.

By questioning the organization of power, power itself is questioned. The history of the United States provided a number of exceptions to the simple historical acceptance of hierarchical order, including the founding's establishment of modern republicanism. Far too often overlooked is the Populist Era at the end of the 19th century. One of American history's profoundest democratic discussions about the organization of power was conducted by the Populists. They experienced the end of the distributed agrarian republic, replaced by the centralized industrial corporate state of today. Politically, the distributed democratic power of the yeoman farm and its numerous associations were replaced by the concentrated, centralized, oligarchical power of the industrial mega-corporation.

Inherently, industrialization is consolidation. It is the consolidation of resources, energy, and labor. Looking at industrialization's brief two century history, its organization has fostered centralized power structures whether in the United States, Germany, the Soviet Union, or most recently China. However, unlike the other three, American industrialization grew out of what had been a brief but significant distributed political order. The Populists were an organized movement who understood industrialization was ripping power from their hands.

In *Democratic Promise*, seminal democratic historian Lawrence Goodwyn writes,

> "Populists dissented against the progressive society that was emerging in the 1890's because they thought that the mature corporate state would, unless restructured, erode the democratic promise of America. Not illogically, therefore, they sought to redesign certain central components in the edifice of American capitalism."

Most essentially, the Populists understood control of technology, the telegraph and railroads used by the banks to organize and consolidate the money system and markets, were integral to reordering power.

> "The agrarian reformers attempted to overcome a system of finance capitalism that was rooted in Eastern commercial banks and which radiated outward through trunk-line railroad networks to link in a number of common purposes of America's consolidating corporate community. ...As John D. Rockefeller had conclusively demonstrated in the course of creating the Standard Oil Trust, railroad networks were a central ingredient both in the combination movement itself and in the political corruption that grew out of monopoly." (Goodwyn)

In response to this new societal organization initiated by the new corporate structure and industrial technologies, the Populists realized their inherited political traditions offered few answers.

> "James Murdock of the *Progressive Farmer* also located the cause of widespread hardship in the political backwardness of the

nation's leaders and party system. 'We are in the era of steam, railroad, telegraph and mammoth machinery. The financial system that answered to the age of the slow coach, sickle and spinning wheel will not respond to this. We have had a revolution in manufactures and transportation, and we must have a radical change in our financial system.'" (Goodwyn)

The Populists tried addressing these challenges in numerous ways, first creating the Farmers Alliance to collectively and democratically organize the independent farmers. They conceived a new money system, the Sub-Treasury plan with local banks distributedly located across the country, not consolidated in several cities on the East Coast. Money would in part be based on the farmers' land and crops, an exponentially more sound foundation than any crypto currency. Finally, the Populists entered the electoral political arena.

"The substance of the third party's experiment in a new political language for an industrial society was the belief that government had fallen disastrously behind the sweeping changes of industrial society, leaving the mass of the people as helpless victims of outmoded rules." (Goodwyn)

In the end, organizationally, they were incapable of matching the growing power of the corporation and industrial technology.

"The collapse of Populism meant, in effect, that the cultural values of the corporate state were politically unassailable in twentieth-century America... The 'money question' passed out of American politics essentially through self-censorship. This result, quite simply, was a product of cultural intimidation. In its broader implications, however, the silencing of debate about 'concentrated capital' betrayed a fatal loss of nerve on the part of those who, during Populism, dared to speak in the name of a people's movement." (Goodwyn)

The first move of any new established power is to end discussion about the organization of their power. The Populists had this discussion, a discussion about how democracy could survive a new technological era. For their efforts, they have basically been written out of American history, disappeared along with any discussion about the money system, but even more importantly any acknowledgment of the role technology plays in establishing political order. Any understanding of technology as politics disappeared with them just as industrial technology fundamentally reshaped the 20th century.

Across the 20th century, a handful of thinkers attempted to explore the political implications of technology, yet their thought remained largely insignificant in denting the schools of economic thought, the culturally dominant political thinking established to shape and value industrial society, a thinking that ignored the political basics of industrial organization, most especially the power of the corporation.

The very real politics of technology became insignificant in relation to the mystical, deified forces of supply and demand. It is not an accident that thinkers such as Thorstein Veblen, Norbert Wiener, Marshall McLuhan, Jane Jacobs, Lewis Mumford, Ivan Illich and others remain largely unknown, their thinking of insignificant influence. Together, they laid a path to develop a politics of technology: a school of thought essential to in any way understand or shape human affairs of the 21st century.

In the Western tradition, beginning with the Greeks, it is thought that a greater understanding of the world, knowledge, was always a virtue. This Greek ethos laid the foundation of Western scientific thought. Two thousand years after the Greeks, a renaissance of Greek thought combined with Europe's adoption of Indian numbers and Arab math, sparked the Scientific Revolution. The Ancient Greek ethos that all knowledge was a virtue forcefully reasserted itself, directly transferring itself to the development of technology. Just as it was thought more knowledge was an unmitigated good, so too the ability to create any given technology was accepted uncritically. By the 20th century, technological development became exclusively valued by culturally dominant industrial economic values, capitalist or socialist, with little or no understanding that every technology asserted values of the technology itself.

One of the greatest early critics of developing 20th century economics, Thorstein Veblen, in *The Place of Science in Modern Civilization* (1919), understood the uncritical acceptance of unlimited knowledge as a virtue hindered the ability to critically analyze technology. He wrote,

> "This is the one secure holding-ground of latter-day conviction, that 'the increase and diffusion of knowledge among men' is indefeasibly right and good. When seen in such perspective as will clear it of the trivial perplexities of workday life, this proposition is not questioned within the horizon of the western culture, and no other cultural ideal holds a similar unquestioned place in the convictions of civilized mankind."

Veblen wrote as industrial technologies fundamentally shifted the shape of life in America. He correctly tied the unquestioned virtue of unlimited knowledge to the development of industrial technology and the culture it was creating. In a speech four decades later, one of the founders of the new era of quantum technology, nuclear physicist and technologist, J. Robert Oppenheimer noted "the phrase the ethical neutrality of science must be a fairly empty one, as an occupation it is based on a very clear belief that is good to know."

Veblen explains the inability to develop critical science and thus a sophisticated value of technology, leads to what he calls a "matter-of-fact" system of technological development. This is the same understanding communications scientist Norbert Wiener addressed in 1948 using the term "know-how." In both cases it is the simplistic engineer's appraisal of technological development as a process of A + B = C. Such an exclusive process, Veblen and Wiener similarly conclude, eventually leads to technology developed exclusively for the sake of technology. Veblen writes,

> "But the canons of validity under whose guidance he [scientists and technologists] works are those imposed by the modern

technology, through habituation to its requirements; and therefore his results are available for the technological purpose. His canons of validity are made for him by the cultural situation; they are habits of thought imposed on him by the scheme of life current in the community in which he lives; and under modern conditions this scheme of life is largely machine-made. In the modern culture, industry, industrial processes, and industrial products have progressively gained upon humanity, until these creations of man's ingenuity have latterly come to take the dominant place in the cultural scheme; and it is not too much to say that they have become the chief force in shaping men's daily life, and therefore the chief factor in shaping men's habits of thought. Hence men have learned to think in the terms in which the technological processes act. This is particularly true of those men who by virtue of a peculiarly strong susceptibility in this direction become addicted to that habit of matter-of-fact inquiry that constitutes scientific research."

A few years later, the great thinker on technology, Marshall McLuhan, would more succinctly put Veblen's above observation: first we shape technology and then technology shapes us. In refusing to acknowledge a politics of technology, *Homo sapiens* becomes a product of technology.

Politically, industrial and now quantum technologies produce greater and greater centralization of political, economic, and cultural power. In 1950, *Brave New World* author Aldous Huxley writes in his essay *Science, Liberty, and Peace,*

"James Mill believed that, when everybody had learned to read, the reign of reason and democracy would be assured forever. But in actual historical fact the spread of free compulsory education, and, along with it, the cheapening and acceleration of the older methods of printing, have almost everywhere been followed by an increase in the power of ruling oligarchies at the expense of the masses."

To "older methods of printing" we now add broadcast media, digital communications, and their resulting technology oligarchies. Huxley warns, "Progressive technology has persuaded the many that concentration of political and economic power is for the general benefit."

Huxley writes industrial technology based exclusively on economic values facilitates centralization:

"There has been more money in working for the mass producers and mass distributors; and the mass producers and mass distributors have had more money because financiers have seen that there was more profit for them, and more power, in a centralized than in a decentralized system of production."

A quarter century later, Goodwyn wrote:

"The more germane historical reality is that centralization of American farmland had occurred even before corporate farming could prove or disprove its relative 'efficiency.' It was simply a matter of capital and the power of those having capital to prevent remedial democratic legislation."

The development of economics has not been that of a science, but simply descriptions and justifications of the processes of industrialization. Its laws have more in common with the declarations of ancient priests upholding the rule of kings and emperors than any relationship to describing a natural force such as gravity. The silence in economics on the role of technology is deafening. Just as the Populists and Veblen, Huxley concludes our inability to devise a political understanding of technology gradually gives technology control of future development:

"For the present, Western societies remain at the mercy of their progressive technologies, to the intense discomfort of everybody concerned. Man as a moral, social and political being is sacrificed to *homo faber*, or man the smith, the inventor and forger of new gadgets. ...so long as the results of pure science are applied for the purpose of making our system of mass-producing and mass-distributing industry more expensively elaborate and more highly specialized, there can be nothing but ever greater centralization of power in ever fewer hands. And the corollary of this centralization of economic and political power is the progressive loss by the masses of their civil liberties, their personal independence and their opportunities for self-government."

Our inability, more accurately our refusal, to develop a politics of technology has led to completely unaccountable technological development. In 1970, seminal politics of technology thinker Ivan Illich explained in *Tools of Conviviality* the inevitable path we've trotted, again a path the Populists clearly viewed almost a century before. Illich writes,

"Society can be destroyed when further growth of mass production renders the milieu hostile, when it extinguishes the free use of the natural abilities of society's members, when it isolates people from each other and locks them into a man-made shell, when it undermines the texture of community by promoting extreme social polarization and splintering specialization, or when cancerous acceleration enforces social change at a rate that rules out legal, cultural, and political precedents as formal guidelines to present behavior. Corporate endeavors which thus threaten society cannot be tolerated. At this point it becomes irrelevant whether an enterprise is nominally owned by individuals, corporations, or the state, because no form of management can make such fundamental destruction serve a social purpose."

He sums up both capitalist and socialist industrial politics:

"People tend to relinquish the task of envisaging the future to a professional elite. They transfer power to politicians who

9

promise to build up the machinery to deliver this future. They accept a growing range of power levels in society when inequality is needed to maintain high outputs. Political institutions themselves become draft mechanisms to press people into complicity with output goals."

Illich concludes, "Our present ideologies are useful to clarify the contradictions which appear in a society which relies on the capitalist control of industrial production; they do not, however, provide the necessary framework for analyzing the crisis in the industrial mode of production itself."

Here is the key. In analyzing the "industrial mode of production itself," you need to analyze the technology itself. Our present political and social ideologies are not simply insufficient, but cripplingly tied to the past and detrimentally entrenched across society. Organizational understanding is crippled by the default order of hierarchy. Centralized control is perceived as the exclusive political method of organization. In contradiction, Illich, along with Veblen, Wiener, and Huxley, understood we needed to reassess our relation to science, most especially in regards to the future of humanity and technological development: science offers no future inevitabilities.

"The vision of new possibilities requires only the recognition that scientific discoveries can be useful in at least two opposite ways. The first leads to specialization of functions, institutionalization of values and centralization of power and turns people into the accessories of bureaucracies or machines. The second enlarges the range of each person's competence, control, and initiative, limited only by other individuals' claims to an equal range of power and freedom." (Illich)

Huxley similarly concluded, "There is nothing in the results of disinterested scientific research which makes it inevitable that they should be applied for the benefit of centralized finance, industry and government." Today, science is used to constrain thought and validate centralized control. Veblen suggests a more holistic view of the implementation of science, one understanding science's cultural roots: "Such positive action may be classified under two heads: (*a*) action which takes its start in politics, to end in the field of science: and (*b*) action which takes its start in science, to end in politics."

Thus, a group of 20th century thinkers understood science and technology had political implications, implications many scientists and technologists have not simply ignored but denied; most never even considered it. Our inability to evolve politics has led to an increasing centralization of power, a centralization more and more led by the demands of technology itself.

In recorded human history, centralized hierarchical order is the dominant organization of power across human society. Hierarchy has long been wrongly characterized as the "natural" order of power. Nature was repeatedly misinterpreted across history to validate centralized power much in the same way 20th century economics justified the concentrated power of the corporation. Physical power (most essentially the power to inflict one's will through organized violence) became essential to hierarchical organization. Power backed romanticized notions of lions as the king of beasts, with little understanding the complexity of ecological systems. Power celebrated social dominance through physicality, ironically in a species overwhelmingly defined by information and communication. This simplistic and crude structuring of social order was detrimental and grows ever more destructive as technology became more powerful. In his *A Primate's Memoir,* neurologist Robert Sapolsky notes if a troop of baboons relied on the physically dominant male for finding food sources they would starve. Such order, the living knowledge within the troop, was provided by old females, the antithesis of a physically imposed dominant young male hierarchy.

Many of today's hierarchical traditions trace back ten-thousand years to what remains one of humanity's greatest technological eras, the domestication of plants and animals and the beginning of the Agrarian Age. This was a significant advance in human knowledge along with a growth in the quantity of information necessary to conduct daily human life. Previous to the Agrarian Era, humanity's several hundred-thousand years as hunter-gatherers, knowledge/information was largely equally distributed. Elements of life impacted a given social group simultaneously. There was no great advantage or even an ability to store or control information outside the person. Just as with a baboon troop, knowledge beyond daily occurrence was stored in memory, giving older persons a degree of social standing.

With the Agrarian Era, knowledge and information increased, most essentially the knowledge of the right times to sow and reap. The first science was gained from an understanding of the movement of the moon, planets, and stars. Control of the resulting calendar became a lever of power. Gradually, agrarian societies producing excess food-stuffs allowed greater and greater concentrations of population. With this concentration came ever more sophisticated social organization, requiring more information and communication. The ability to order this information and communication were used as levers to establish hierarchical, centralized control. In return, organized central power — culturally, politically and economically — justified the centralized organization of power.

Ancient Greek thinking laid the foundation to what eventually developed into the scientific method. Oppenheimer noted the Greeks added to human observations of nature a certain rigor, a valuing of the ability to repeat. In looking at the development of our matter-of-fact/know-how preeminent technological ethos, the practice of rigor, the ability to repeat scientific observation was essential to gaining the knowledge and capabilities necessary to create the technology surrounding us. The matter-of-fact/know-how approach, allows a simplistic, part by part understanding, opposed to what is the greater complexity and meaning of any system as a whole. For example, looking only at the kidney in trying to understand the human body or at one species to define the entire ecological system when it is just a part of a whole.

In practice, this "know-how" approach blinds us to greater meaning, automatically constraining our view to largely finding only what we set out to look for. This becomes not simply problematic but detrimental for today's technologically shaped society. The constrained limited know-how used to develop a given technology becomes locked into that technology. As a technology becomes not just a greater part of the society, but an essential force shaping the society, this constraint defines society and restricts future development of technology by both limiting alternative thinking and prejudicing future development to what already exists.

Looking at the established organization of political power and the inclusive interaction between the physical, energy, and information, nothing is more revelatory than America's food system. The beginning of this piece documented the industrialization and consolidation of American agriculture. The resulting present system reveals the physical components, such as concentration of land ownership; tractor, truck, and equipment manufacturers; tied together by roads, railroads, and global grain ships. From an energy perspective, the entire system is soaked in fossil fuels, not simply in powering the tractors or getting harvests to national and global markets, but in the creation of fertilizer, pesticides, and herbicides. A system that went from including over half the population in farming a century ago to today where less than 2% are directly involved.

The system became increasingly information rich, not just in all aspects of organizing this vast consolidated system, but in the knowledge essential for continually changing pesticides and herbicides in response to insects and plants evolving in reaction to their overzealous application. In recent years, control of the engineering of plants and animals at the genetic level creates an ever more essential information component of the system controlled by a handful of corporations seeking greater power over life at one of its most fundamental levels. Finally, a handful of grocery companies deliver the majority of food, a distribution system reliant on the automobile.

With the industrialization of the small farm and resulting population migration to urban areas, organization of physical locality, personal movement, once defined by either foot or horse, was transformed by the automobile. For American life, the car became a seemingly existential necessity. American car culture saw people's economic, political and cultural affairs designed around the car. A handful of automobile companies and oil companies became powers nationally and globally, with smaller companies, responsible for the automobile street infrastructure rising as local powers. The automobile consolidated the distribution of all goods, both necessities and advertising-driven consumption. The pinnacle of centralized automobile distribution came with the suburban mall made possible by automobile-created suburban housing, drawing consumers from miles around, spread across their individual manicured landscapes.

In the last decade, the development of compute information technologies saw the first challenge to the societal organizational hegemony of the automobile. The "Amazon distribution" system challenged the decades-old car model distribution. This new system was made possible by information technologies, by the internet. Instead of stores within relatively short driving distance or massive malls farther spaced, the Amazon model sees numerous large distributed warehouses storing goods. These warehouses are geographically organized to allow a certain efficacy in delivery by trucks moving door to door. Whether this is a more efficient process in regards to energy use than established auto-centric distribution is unclear (I've seen no comparative numbers). However, it is without a doubt far more energy wasteful than a distribution system with the final leg of distribution reliant on the human body unaided by other external energy sources, for example, local stores organized in walking or biking distance.

The second threat to dominant car culture has also been made possible by information/communications technologies. This has been the growth of "remote working," catalyzed by the Covid disruption. This has seen a hollowing out of office centers, themselves creations of the 20th century information wave. It has not yet seen a corresponding reorganization of other social activities based around the increased presence of individuals in their homes. For the most part it has only led to a greater increase in online communication, handing ever more power to tech-information companies.

The Amazon distribution model and work at home movement reveal the increasingly dominant role information technologies now play shaping both locality and energy use, the manifestation of information. In a relatively short period of time, this reorganization by information technologies has made Amazon massively powerful, a power comprising physical, energy, and information organization. At this point, "internet" is used offhandedly to refer to what is a plethora of networks sharing many of the same technical standards, but nonetheless separately organized. For example, the internal network of a corporation may run through the internet with its internal communication and data "walled-off" from the outside. Customers place their data on centralized corporate controlled servers, euphemistically marketed as "the cloud," now including centralized compute power marketed as AI, all connected via the internet. Increasingly, the engineered internet has more in common with the old mainframe model of central server and dumb terminals than any massively distributed network as first promoted. The networks are engineered both internally and in their connections to society's greater physical and social structures, facilitating further central control. Thus, there is the power of the networks' actual organization and the power of how the networks connect to what is increasingly every aspect of society.

Today, America's once largely distributed yeoman farm republic is now an industrial, centralized, increasingly information rich, corporate oligarchy. The exceptional order of distributed democracy is now entirely replaced by traditional hierarchical organization wielding new tools.

In the last century and half, starting with the biology of Charles Darwin's natural selection and continuing with relativity and quantum physics, an antithetical view of centralized order came to be better understood. A universe not of centralized, hierarchical, top-down order, but one infinitely distributed, networked, and dynamically interacting. Order rose not from a powerful centralized top but through innumerable interactions at multidimensional levels. As an analogy to social organization, it is order much more resembling historically exceptional democracy than our entrenched traditional hierarchy.

In a wonderful book, *Metazoa: Animal Life and the Birth of the Mind,* University of Sydney Professor Peter Godfrey-Smith looks at the organization inherent in all life. From the beginning of life on this planet, every single celled organism, the biggest dinosaurs of a hundred million years ago, and ourselves today have been organized by information and the processes of communicated information. Smith makes a sublime association between objective, naturally engineered organization, and the subjective meaning of communication. He writes, "Point of view has always been metaphorical, but it suggests a lot of integration." By integration he is talking about the organization of any organism in its abilities to process information. This organization can be separate, done through different channels or integrated, where information flows together, internally. "Many animals are only partially integrated."

When an organism's inherent organization separates the streams of information, what it collects from various senses,

> "You tend to gain some things—often you may gain speed—and lose some things. If sensory streams are separated from each other, you lose the ability to combine different kinds of information that might be useful when considered together, like the many premises of an argument or many pieces of a puzzle. If you allow different parts of yourself to perform their own actions, you risk a situation where your active parts want to do contradictory things. In the extreme, you risk fragmenting entirely, into sub-agents who see their own scenes and make their own decisions. That certainly looks like a bad idea, but we should not assume that everything follows a shape with a central CEO and a lot of underlings."

This separation of sensory channels can be looked at as analogous to the organizational model for modern human society from Adam Smith's division of labor to the extreme specialization at the top of academia. By organizing specialization and division, we socially engineer subjectivity. Society — life itself! — is seen and experienced through very narrow informational bands with little integration. With the power of the modern mega-corporation and centralized government, we attempt, (and increasingly fail) to tie things together under CEOs, whether as heads of giant corporations or presidents in white houses. Such institutions and people are parts of failing hierarchies, unnatural orders incapable of effectively tying things together, much less to (in any aesthetic way) integrate the multifarious channels that comprise societal order. This organization overwhelmingly breeds prejudiced subjectivity; the semantics of all information communicated limited in its interpretation.

We hold larger centralized nervous systems (biological engineering to process both quantity and quality of sensational information) as indicators of greater intelligence. Of course, such valuing places ourselves at a subjective top. Godfrey-Smith writes,

> "Octopus embody a design very different from our own. The octopus nervous system is decentralized; about two thirds of the neurons are not in the brain (itself a vaguely defined region), but the arms, especially in the upper arms. These act not just as outlying sensors and relay systems feeding the central brain; there is an apparent delegation of the control of some motions to the arms themselves."

The octopus upsets our wrongful prejudice of the necessity of a centralized hierarchical brain.

> "A decentralization of the body's controllers is seen not only in the octopus. Forms of it are found in many animals, including ourselves, and there are reasons why this might be expected to some extent. The features of animals that are responsible for sensing and action, the features whose history I have been charting, are complicated and require many parts. Organized arrays of cells are needed for seeing, other arrays of cells are needed to produce movement, and nervous systems with still more cells are needed to coordinate it all. Once you have all this machinery, you have some new evolutionary options. You can separate out some pathways, create local lines of control. It becomes a choice, in an evolutionary sense, whether you create separate streams that control action or integrate everything into a single stream. You can also do a bit of both; you can have largely separate tracks with some cross-talk between them." (Godfrey-Smith)

Godfrey-Smith documents life as organization, every aspect of it from a single cell to the complex nervous system of the octopus. With organization, the engineering defines how information is processed, from which is derived semantics.

Looking not at organisms, but at the body politic, organization is just as essential to how we process information. Organization designed by information to process other information. Godfrey-Smith writes, all organization determines future possibilities. In this still new technological era, the control of nascent information technologies by a handful of massive corporations using centralized networks coordinated by massive data "centers" limits our ability for future options. Politically, these new centrally controlled information systems make democracy impossible.

Using knowledge gained from 20th century physics, humanity innovated compute technology and the transistor leading to an exponential increase in information and communication. Norbert Wiener, the great 20th century thinker on information systems, stated, "Information is information, not matter or energy." Like much physics, we define information more in what it does, in know-how, as opposed to know-what. Matter, energy, and information are intertwined in all aspects of human existence, essential components of all life. At the beginning of the 20th century, Einstein revealed energy and matter to be equivalent. A small amount of matter consisted of inconceivable quantities of energy. To manifest and be utilized, information must take the form of energy or matter — an essential understanding for any politics of information technology.

Information has always been at the core of defining *Homo sapiens.* As social beings, communication – the transference of information – is essential to who and what we are. The control of information and its communication has been a key component of all hierarchy across human history. Nonetheless, our definition of information remains rather nebulous.

In his introduction to Claude Shannon's *The Mathematical Theory of Communication,* Warren Weaver sums up Shannon's thinking, "Just as the amount of information in a system is a measure of its degree of organization, so the entropy of a system is a measure of its degree of disorganization; and the one is simply the negative of the other." Shannon's math underlies the structure and processes of all recent information/communication technologies. Most intriguing and valuable is the idea that information is valued through its organization. Whether as energy or matter, this information organization is accomplished via communication.

Shannon states, "The semantic aspects of communication are irrelevant to the engineering aspects." Using this definition, control of information has two aspects. One is the actual structures of communication: the engineering. The second is the meaning: the semantics. The former is objective, while the latter always contains elements of subjectivity. While the engineering of communication can be straightforwardly conceived, the meaning derived from what's communicated much less so, no matter how much effort those in control attempt to restrict meaning.

Both the engineered structure and semantics are politics. In both respects, this bifurcated control of information has been fundamental to the organization of family, tribe, nation, and empire. In hierarchical order, communication is engineered to allow a small centralized top control of an exponentially larger bottom. This is the objective communication structure of oligarchy, monarchy, and tyranny. Democracy requires more distributed communication order. The Greek and Roman citizen assemblies, the distributed level system of the American republic from local to federal, the Bill of Rights' declaration of freedom of the press, are all examples of objectively engineered distributed communication organization. Such openly engineered systems are fundamental to any notion of self-government. The organization of the processes, technologies, and institutions of communication are essential politics, regardless of any and all ideas passed through them.

Reviving democracy would require a complete reorganization of society, an engineered redistribution of power. Simultaneously, the increasing adoption of technologies based on a greater knowledge of the distributed order of nature, such as information technologies, genetic manipulation, and the latest mad rush to nuclear power in both weaponry and energy production to power an exponential increase in centralized compute power, makes centralized control not simply politically problematic, but raises serious questions about its ability to control the technology itself in regards to stability and viability.

Wiener's insight that information is neither energy nor matter, combined with the understanding that information manifests itself in human experience in its ability to organize energy and matter, is a valuable starting point for thinking about restructuring politics. At its most fundamental level, human society organizing matter and energy is politics. Rethinking political organization begins with understanding social organization which includes the organization of matter, energy, and information.

Democracy is the most useful organizational and processing system for a human society awash with what for the individual might as well be infinite quantities of information, quantities making it simply impossible for an individual to grasp, much less process. Democratic politics need a distributed structured system, a system having more in common with the participatory systems of Athens and Rome than the representative system of modern republicanism. A system where a central meeting place for the entire citizen body, such as Roman forum or the Athenian *ekklesia,* isn't necessary, but we might consider a system where innumerable smaller participatory nodes are networked together via multiple channels, allowing both deliberation and action by the nodes and the individuals comprising them.

All politics begins with local geographic characteristics. *Homo sapiens* remain biological organisms shaped by the environments they inhabit. The planet we collectively inhabit is composed of local areas of both advantageous and disadvantageous characteristics. Industrialization flattened out many of these disparate characteristics, creating homogenization. Industrial technology allowed a radical overriding of locality, for example creating a similar technologically produced environment whether you lived in the suburbs of Boston, Phoenix, or Seattle. In fact, traveling the world, you can find similar or exactly the same daily living conditions – climate control, automobile centered transport, diet, and entertainment – provided by the same corporations, whether living in Lagos, Tokyo, Rome, Lima, or Moscow.

Can we instead apply the knowledge we've learned over the last century of nature's distributed order to our societal order – cultural, political, economic and technological? Reorganizing literally from the ground up, society's physical, energy, and information components, a reorganization incorporating an understanding all such structures are politics. We still have an enormously limited understanding of distributed order, a still greatly undeveloped notion of possible democratic order, an understanding with no sense of the importance of technology. Democratic order needs continuous, egalitarian communication between all elements. Evolving democracy requires the purposeful distributed networked organization of the physical, energy, and information, and an intertwining across innumerable networks comprising all three.

The composition of such networks would be people organized into a variety of associations – cultural, political, and economic. These associations would function as nodes of massive globally connected distributed networks. Foundationally, these associations would be locally defined, incorporating the advantages and disadvantages of the local elements of geography, weather, and ecology. They would take into account how a person physically interacts with these elements and just as importantly how each person in a given locality interacts with other people – culturally, politically, and economically.

The fundamental structure of democracy is face to face meetings where information is directly communicated and discussed from individual to individual or individual to group or group to group. It also includes organization of the production and the distribution of necessities, such as food and clothing. A purposeful physical organization facilitating communication between individuals and their physical activities such as gathering together or picking up necessities where a person can walk or bicycle using the least amount of exogenous energy. As Illich in maybe his most sublime insight noted, "Participatory democracy demands low-energy technology, and free people must travel the road to productive social relations at the speed of a bicycle."

Key to understanding the above paragraph are the relationships between people without intervening media. All media – Webster: "something in a middle position" – intrudes some organization of power. Obviously this doesn't mean democracy requires civilization without media; in fact, for better and worse, what we conceive of civilization is media. However, the naked individual as a member of whatever human organization is the most fundamental level of power, where each member of any combined social organization has equal say in any group decision is elementary democracy. The placing of any and all media between individuals and groups always adds another element of power. The organization of the medium itself and how the people interact with the medium always add elements of power. If the social organization with the introduction of any medium is to be democratic, both the medium and resulting organization need to be democratically structured.

Distributed networked nodes can be permanently structured together, defined geographically such as all nodes around a lake, a river basin, those sharing a desert plain, or regionally created with the assistance of various media in the case of neighborhoods of a city. These associations can also form temporary coalitions, such as cities working collectively together creating and connecting to greater energy and transportation infrastructures, a fundamentally different process for example than the present process where cities in the US need to work at the state or federal levels to act together. Here state and federal organization become media intruding their own power, often overriding the power of the locality. Instead, associations can be of countless varieties distributedly connected not simply by location, but for all issues of concern, order can be provided without centralization. Order is defined in the connections.

Whatever the concerns of any given node and network, the creation, editing, and communication of information will be a primary concern. Today, as the individual is drowned in a tsunami of information, it is impossible for any person to utilize information in all but an extremely limited, a specialized sense. Outside individuals comprising the divided specialized professions, "experts," be they a lawyer, doctor, or engineer and the information they are directly able to manipulate, overwhelmingly all people are simply consumers of information. All individuals, including the specialized, are powerless in regards to news of their communities, nations, and the planet. This is a result of both the centralized architecture of the new compute technologies and the entrenched industrial order which allows no participation outside specialized inputs and mass consumption.

An important note here needs to be made about consumption. There is no argument industrialization created a cornucopia of consumer stuff, both necessities and more than plenty not so necessaries. While control of the production processes was overwhelmingly centralized, there is without a doubt a certain democratic element to mass consumption. As the sublime Modern artist Andy Warhol quipped, "Everyone drinks the same Coke." However, this essay is concerned not simply with the product of consumption, but who controls and decides what and how things are produced, most especially what is the role of the individual in these processes. A revival of politics where the role of the individual is not simply a cog in production with the only reward consumption, but as a decision maker helping design the life they live.

Just as a hundred thousand years ago, the individual was reliant on their social group for survival, today every individual relies on organization to make any sense of the data deluge. However, the processes providing useful information are overwhelmingly hierarchically controlled, from Federal bureaucracies to massive corporations like Microsoft, Google, Amazon, and Facebook, or any number of industrial corporations. The ever more powerful information conglomerates now seek to automate decision processes, marketed as AI, removing individual control and simultaneously entrenching existing power, resulting in unprecedented prejudicial control of the future.

The Agrarian Age saw the reorganization of the physical environment, of locality, as society's greatest mover. The Industrial Era witnessed the mass harnessing of energy to reshape and homogenize society. Both were reliant on information to manifest. In each of these eras, shaped by new technologies, human activity radically changed: first from hunter-gatherers to farmers, then from farmers to factory laborers. Now in the era of compute technologies, humanity spends more time creating, processing, communicating, and acting on information. Certainly, if it continues on the course established, and that is doubtful for a number of reasons including energy needs and systemic stability, centrally controlled automation will grow. In opposition, people can be directly organized into the process, both as individuals and as collective democratic associations, organized around creating, editing, and communicating information, and most essentially deciding.

Just as the main concern of the Agrarian Era individual was farming, the laborer of the Industrial Era, this Information Era will require individual concern, identity, in today's popular and not so insightful political parlance, in the creating, editing, and communicating information. In this regard, people need to be valued for their informational roles without devaluing both their roles and the information by necessitating monetization as the only means to provide value. During the Agrarian Era, the vast majority of people were valued not monetarily, but by their roles in society as farmer, merchant, or craftsperson. Industrialism manufactured the overwhelmingly dominant and almost exclusive societal valuing through monetization. There is no need to monetize most information. New values need to develop, including valuing every individual as a creator, editor, and communicator of information. Money itself needs to become a more information rich medium.

Many of these values will be created, learned, and their merit accessed through the organization itself, most essentially via participation. Elections are essential to democracy. They are a non-monetary valuing system, one of few left existing today, though it's very difficult to look at today's money bought, reality television election process as a system providing any democratic value.

One part of the present system that can be exponentially expanded is the jury system. The jury system goes back at least two and half thousand years to the Ancient Greeks. Juries can be vastly expanded to make all systems more accountable, bringing back a form of the Ancient Athenian accountability system of *euthenya*. This was the process begun after any magistrate held office. It was an auditing, both fiscal and procedural, to hold account the magistrate's actions in office.

All magistrates served only one year, most selected by lot. In modern republicanism, elections were thought to provide accountability, but have proved completely insufficient. Our mega-corporations, it is preached by our economist priesthood, are supposedly held to account through markets or via government regulation, systems the corporations control. Such unaccountability makes the fundamentally undemocratic structure and processes of contemporary power crystal clear. The most elementary process separating democracy from tyranny is holding power accountable. If power isn't accountable, there is no self-government.

A model of the jury system can be expanded to include interpretation of all laws, replacing the far too dominant judicial process now run by judges, most egregiously represented by the unelected nine member Supreme Court and their thunderous marbled hall proclamations of order. Instead a widely distributed jury system would be an organization seeking to make law more dynamic, not that of traditional hierarchical law seeking to be permanently etched in stone, but more similar to the dynamic interaction of living systems. "Information is even more a matter of process than a matter of storage." (Wiener)

Information and its communication must be freed from constraints of corporate ownership, such as patents and copyrights, and not stored lifeless in massive data bases, but allowed to live dynamically across multitudes of associations with their actions and in the very organization of the networks they form. An evolved jury system can be looked at as decision making bodies, part of associations valuing information based on precise content and allowing decisions to be made on this information.

Imagining such change immediately envisions much greater complexity, yet it is a complexity inherent in the organization of nature and, importantly, increasingly in the technology we create. In creating distributed networked systems, another recent scientific discovery may be the most important. The process of feedback must be engineered into all democratic structures. Feedback is defined here as a simple return of information based on information communicated or an action taken.

Norbert Wiener was one of the first to understand the importance feedback played as an essential element for life systems and to understand it would be an imperative component of any automated system. Wiener states, "It is certainly true that the social system is an organization like the individual, that it is bound together by a system of communication, and that it has a dynamics in which circular processes of a feedback nature play an important part." Feedback is an imperative part of all political systems. No political system, no matter how autocratic, survives without feedback. However oligarchic/tyrannical power structures have massive channels of communication transmitting from the top, their feedback channels narrow and extremely limited. Just as importantly, feedback in such centralized systems are not valued for change, but for tamping or stomping down dissent of the established order. In a distributed network, feedback becomes essential for order, channels of return are equal in volume and force as those initiating the signal, be it information or an action.

Distributed networks are much more dynamic, capable of quickly enacting and reacting to signals sent and actions taken. Such networks are basically alive, quite the opposite of centralized industrial systems where for example feedback to the changes wrought on ecological systems were largely absent or ignored. Our archaic systems of government, encased in cold marble, where the past is worshiped, not utilized, can evolve into dynamic living systems meeting the unending challenges and the joy and tragedy of life.

"The Populists had dared to pursue cultural acceptance of a democratic politics open to serious structural evolution of the society."

— LAWRENCE GOODWYN

"The most socially desirable power of a tool can only be the outcome of political procedure."

— IVAN ILLICH

"The political importance of the township was never grasped by the founders, and that the failure to incorporate it into either the federal or the state constitutions was 'one of the tragic oversights of post-revolutionary political development'."

— HANNAH ARENDT, *ON REVOLUTION*, 1963

Across the globe, politics grows increasingly impotent to meet the challenges humanity faces in the 21st century. Our political institutions are archaic, while politics inherent in all organization are largely ignored or placed in stringent categories considered nonpolitical. Today, politics' greatest deficiency is an incredible ignorance of the role technology plays in shaping society, despite the fact from *Homo sapiens* rise on the African continent, our growing knowledge and the resulting technology shaped our lives.

In the last two centuries, the growth of human knowledge about nature's order has grown exponentially. This expansion of scientific knowledge led to an explosion of powerful technologies with the Industrial Revolution. Our ability to harness the power of burning fossil fuels changed the landscape of the planet, reorganizing human life and the ecologies shaping us more than anything since the Agrarian revolution ten thousand years before.

Simultaneous with the Industrial Revolution, though in no way cause and effect, was the birth of modern republicanism with the founding of the United States. This political order was based on the agrarian culture about to be largely swept aside as industrialism arose to dominate. While republican institutions, always anomalies in recorded human history, were radical in their reintroduction in opposition to then established monarchical order, however, they proved completely insufficient to meet the onslaught of change introduced by industrial technologies.

With industrialization came a resurgence in the modern republic of the very old human tradition of reliance on centralized hierarchical order, most especially with industrialism's only real social innovation — the corporation. The reintroduction of republicanism created a revolutionary political atmosphere for two centuries across the planet's agrarian cultures. Yet, the distributed order of modern republicanism was largely still-birthed. Politics increasingly became about swapping out the top of largely or exclusively ordered hierarchical systems to pull already established levers of power in the name of change.

This fight for the centralized top was best exemplified with the 20th century communist revolutions, the only political ideology to be formed, or better malformed, directly from an ideology created by industrialization. Despite both the Union of Soviet Socialist Republics and The People's Republic of China's use of republic in their official names, both quickly adopted centralized rule. However, some Bolsheviks, such as Lenin and Bukharin, also had ideas of a more decentralized order. Ascending to the top of a two and half thousand year old hierarchical civilizational order, Mao understood in thought, certainly not always in deed, all true revolutionary change would mean distributing power. Of course a steel foundry in every backyard may not have been the best leap forward, it was thought wrestling with decentralized industrial order.

The US represented industrialization destroying the agrarian republic, its politics eventually becoming nothing more than a personal fight over who controls Washington DC, even worse an obsession with who controls the White House.

Now a new information/communication/compute technology revolution upsets the established hierarchies of industrialism and the remaining older hierarchies of agrarianism. However, these technologies are not used to create a new more distributed order with the knowledge of the physical and biological sciences from which they have been derived. Instead, as with industrialism, this new technology empowers newer, even more centralized hierarchies. Most disconcerting, the centralized control being imposed by this technology is highly questionable in its ability to sustain further technological development or the vitality of the current technology, not even considering its impact on humanity's social order or the health of the planet's ecologies.

In direct opposition to humanity's long deification of technology, we are in need of creating a completely secular and healthy politics of technology. A politics that places humanity above technology, that acknowledges technologies as useful tools. Technology's impact on social organization must be understood and designed to just as great a degree as the know-how responsible for creating the technology itself. The revival of politics requires an accompanying appreciation of the worth of every individual, an understanding designing new social organization needs a democratic structure of distributed power allowing both individual and egalitarian collective initiative.

THE POLITICS OF DEMOCRACY

THE GEOMETRY OF POWER

"Geometry – concerned with the shape of individual objects, spatial relationships among various objects, and the properties of surrounding space."

— ENCYCLOPÆDIA BRITANNICA

Power is like gravity, a curvature of space-time. The more concentrated, the more power warps and influences everything around it. Power is helpfully understood from a geometric perspective. The geometric form of centralized power has largely been depicted as that of a pyramid. Paradoxically, the top of the pyramid has the least mass, though it exerts the most influence. To understand centralized political power, an understanding of the shape and properties of networks is also necessary. Centralized power is always simplistically networked. Wide channels of communication flow forcefully in one direction, very narrow feedback channels fitfully return information. With unsymmetrical structure, hierarchical systems of power are by necessity rigid, not only zealously conservative of the established forms they rely upon, but incapable of change, even when it's in power's own greatest self-interest.

Across history, most political thinking is devoid of the simple understanding of the geometry of power, the absence is no mystery. The vast majority of recorded history saw power overwhelmingly centralized, exceptions few. Established power always loathes close examination of structure. The Greeks and Romans both understood the geometry of centralized power. The Greeks called it tyranny, antithetical to self-government, whether defined using the Greek term – democracy, or Rome's Latin – republican. Both understood with self-government, power needed to be both distributed and wherever collected, held for only a brief period of time – the geometric space-time of democracy.

The great democratic thinker Alexis de Tocqueville understood better than most the geometry of power. In the *Ancien Regime et la Revolution,* he explained centralized power was both the cause and then the failure of the 1789 revolution. At the end of the 18th century, he records how all power in France was concentrated under the monarchy,

"The central power in eighteenth-century France... had already succeeded in destroying all the intermediate authorities and, since nothing but a huge and empty space had emerged, from a distance central government appeared to each citizen to be the only means of maintaining the social machine, the single necessary agent of public life."

He continues explaining power's gravitational pull,

"As Paris became more and more the model of the arbiter of taste, the only center of power and the arts, the chief home of national activity, so the industrial life of the nation retreated and concentrated its forces there even more."

In comparison to his contemporaries and really most European political thought since and all contemporary American political thought today, if anything can be so labeled, the great advantage Tocqueville possessed was his experience with and understanding of the 1830s American republic. In contrast to France and the role of Paris he writes,

> "No American citizen imagines that the people of New York could decide the fate of the Union. Furthermore, no one in the state of New York itself imagines that the individual will of the city could by itself manage affairs."

Tocqueville points to this ignorance of the geometry of power and the resulting impotence to effect change, a political affliction shared by France's revolutionaries and manifesting all political thought today,

> "The aims recommended by the reformers were many and varied but their methods were the same. They wanted to borrow the strength of central government and use it to smash everything and rebuild according to a new plan of their own conception. Such a task could, they thought, be accomplished only by the central power."

A half-century later, Tocqueville concludes the revolution's contradiction in result,

> "Let us cease to be surprised at the marvelous ease with which centralization was re-established in France at the beginning of the century. The men of '89 had overturned the building but its foundations had stayed in the very hearts of its destroyers and, upon these foundations, they were able to rebuild it, constructing it more stoutly than it had ever been before."

The historical influence of the two great revolutions of the 18th century remains fascinating. The French Revolution became a fetish, a supposed fount of wisdom for many, including Marx's followers, who with their ascension to power advocated such ludicrous notions as dictatorships of the proletariat. A complete ignorance of the geometry of power resulted in innumerable wrong-headed ideas that were DOA. Centralized power's very shape excluded notions of *égalité, fraternité,* and *liberté.* The always distasteful bourgeois fetishizing of the revolution's violence missed Tocqueville's essential point, "Paris had become the master of France and already an army was gathering which was to turn into the master of Paris."

The historical landscape of George III's American colonies was much different than Louis XVI's France. The simple distance between London and her subjects created the space for the much greater freedom of the American colonists turned rebels. The victorious revolutionaries rose out of an infinitely more distributed system of power than most of the revolutionaries in France could ever imagine. Yet, over time, power gradually centralized, attracted ever more to the gravitational pull of a Washington in alliance with economic power ever more concentrated in a handful of increasingly powerful corporations. Since the defeat of the Populists at the end of the 19th century and with the continual loss of democratic forms, American reformers, like their French predecessors, increasingly looked to centralized control as the means to effect change.

Today, the understanding of the geometry of power, once widespread in America, is largely lost to history. As America enters an election year, political power is so centralized, political focus oppressively concentrates on the presidency. Most amusing, if one has the stomach, the current *ancien* holder of the office proclaims he will save democracy, a power in the very best of circumstances the office has no ability to confer, even if its current occupant had any understanding of it. Such politics is devoid of any notion of the geometry of power. Reliance on centralized power produces only greater centralized power, until, as Tocqueville quotes the Marquis de Mirabeau, "The head becomes too big, then the body becomes apoplectic and dies."

ORDERING DEMOCRACY

Looking across history, two periods shine as examples of democratic political evolution fostering tremendous societal advantage. One would be the founding of the American Republic, which proved highly advantageous for the yeoman farm majority until industrialism literally steamrolled the entire political and economic landscape. The second is Ancient Greece, particularly the experience of Athens. Here was birthed what came to be defined ever since as democracy.

The end of the second millennium B.C. saw the decline of the Bronze Age. Greece was the western and northern frontier of the era's great Middle Eastern civilizations — Egypt, Hittites, and other Mesopotamian. Beginning 1200 B.C., the whole region started to decline, the causes are debated. In Greece, the centrally controlled Minoan "palace culture" civilization of Crete and the Aegean islands collapsed. A similar system of monarchy on mainland Greece centered around Mycenae also collapsed. Simultaneously, the eastern and southern Mediterranean civilizations of Egypt, Hittite, and Mesopotamia all floundered.

Over the next several centuries, the collapse of Greece's centralized palace-culture states allowed the creation of distributed Greek city-state civilization. In his excellent *Rise and Fall of Classical Greece*, Josiah Ober succinctly describes the decline of the one era and the beginnings of the new. He writes,

"The collapse that terminated Bronze Age societies in Western Asia was especially severe in Greece—severe enough to overthrow large-scale social order. The collapse eliminated the Bronze Age Greek palace economies, along with economic specializations and social relationships based on formalized and asymmetrical exchanges between palace-based patrons and their clients. The collapse also lasted long enough to drown out positive memories of Bronze Age monarchy. The difficult conditions of the era fostered local interdependence along with relatively low levels of political and economic inequality: Everyone was poor, elite control was weak, and the threats of famine and piracy were endemic."

Talk about your disruptions!

This environment fostered the rise of the Greek Classic Era of Sparta, Thebes, Athens and scores of other city-states, creating and growing a civilization whose science, math, literature, philosophy, and politics still live today across not just Greece and Europe, but the entire planet. Ober assesses,

> "Classical Greece is the earliest documented case of 'democratic exceptionalism plus efflorescence'—a historically rare combination of economic, cultural, and political conditions pertaining among developed countries in the contemporary world."

Ober notes while certain technological breakthroughs occurred, importantly the beginning of iron and steel weaponry and other implements, what was most responsible for this civilization and its relatively brief glory—its efflorescence—were cultural, political, and social innovations. He writes,

> "The Greek world was arguably a standout in its development of new public institutions that served to increase the level and value of social cooperation without resort to top-down command and control. Valuable institutional innovations were spurred by high levels of local and interstate competition, and they were spread by the circulation of information and learning."

One great innovation was the creation of the Greek alphabet and resulting development of literary culture. This innovation made capable previously unknown social organization, writing nourished cultural, political, and economic links. Many of our present institutions—political, government, and educational—grew from these Ancient Greek roots, all now wilt. Yet, growing institutional failure brings no acute examination of how they are organized and function. Most disastrously, we throw technology at the failures, technology designed by people with the least historical or political sense, and boy, that's saying something.

Along with this institutional breakdown, America experiences a massive degradation of political and social culture. Market values, overwhelmingly defined by a handful of massive corporations, dominate all aspects of society. Values not accounted for by centrally controlled markets are worth little or nothing at all. We've created a neo-palace-culture. The political value of being a citizen is worthless, its debasement starkly personified by the political class themselves. The value of being a good neighbor, a member of the community, is largely nonexistent.

For the species *Homo sapiens*, political and social value is founded in the merit of reciprocity, an understanding and practice that the actions of any individual in regards to others in some ways, at some points, are accounted either beneficial or detrimental. Reciprocity can only be gained through social and political organization, that is by association. An individual's actions may have a greater impact on the group, not directly on another individual, reciprocity may then be gained indirectly.

The great chronicler of early 19th century American democracy, Alexis de Tocqueville writes, "Sentiments and ideas renew themselves, the heart is enlarged, and the human mind is developed only by the reciprocal action of men upon one another."

Tocqueville observes in the 1830s agrarian American republic, reciprocity lives in the multiplicity and ubiquity of associations—people democratically organizing for a common goal or goals. He notes,

> "Americans of all ages, all conditions, all minds constantly unite. Not only do they have commercial and industrial associations in which all take part, but they also have a thousand other kinds: religious, moral, grave, futile, very general and very particular, immense and very small; Americans use associations to give fetes, to found seminaries, to build inns, to raise churches, to distribute books, to send missionaries to the antipodes; in this manner they create hospitals, prisons, schools."

He concludes,

> "Thus the most democratic country on earth is found to be, above all, the one where men in our day have most perfected

the art of pursuing the object of their common desires in common and have applied this new science to the most objects... In democratic countries the science of association is the mother science; the progress of all the others depends on the progress of that one."

America has lost the science of association, thus too, democracy. Organization is overwhelmingly defined by massive corporations and government, government increasingly dominated by the federal level. Value defined by mega-corporate market culture is limited, largely defined by simple transactions of stuff. This act of buying and selling is a rigid, instantaneous reciprocity. A more valuable reciprocity demands both time and degrees of complexity, defining the character of both individuals and community.

Evolutionary biologist Robert Sapolsky well describes ancient cultural reciprocity,

"In its natural form, human reciprocity is a triumph of comfortably and intuitively doing long-term math with apples and oranges—this guy over here is a superstar hunter; that other guy isn't in his league but has your back if there's a lion around; meanwhile, she's amazing at finding the best mongongo nuts, that older woman knows all about medicinal herbs, that geeky guy remembers the best stories. We know where one another live, the debit columns even out over time, and if someone is really abusing the system, we'll get around to collectively dealing with them."

Today's dominant market values defined through money transactions leave social and political complexity hidden and undervalued. Sapolsky astutely notes,

"We tend to think of market interactions as being the epitome of complexity—finding a literal common currency for an array of human needs and desires in the form of this abstraction called money. But at their core, market interactions represent an impoverishment of human reciprocity."

Sapolsky and Tocqueville agree any society's ability to value reciprocity is based on its value of equality. The only way a society can value equality is to have certain structural equality. Sapolsky states the case,

> "Put simply, cultures with more income inequality have less social capital. Trust requires reciprocity and reciprocity requires equality, whereas hierarchy is about domination and asymmetry. Moreover, a culture highly unequal in material resources is almost always unequal in the ability to pull the strings of power, to have efficacy, to be visible. Almost by definition, you can't have a society with both dramatic income inequality and plentiful social capital."

Two centuries previously, Tocqueville correctly stated democracy faced no greater danger than if its business, industry, and government became centrally controlled. American democracy degraded as political, economic, and cultural power became more and more hierarchically controlled.

A rigorous examination of how current society became so hierarchical and centralized is beyond the scope of this short piece. However, a useful look can be provided on one aspect—specialization—the concentration of one field of study, one craft, one manufacture, or one profession exclusive to all others. Specialization has a long history in human affairs, recognized and extolled in political economist Adam Smith's, *The Wealth of Nations*. Smith points to the "division of labor," dividing and making continuously repetitive any given task in manufacturing, as a key to efficiency. As industry grew, over the next century, this division grew ever more intricate with the addition of fossil fueled powered machinery, one could say reaching a certain art form with Henry Ford's assembly line.

Sanctified by industrial economic organization, applied across the rest of society, the division of labor was at best problematic, and in many ways detrimental, no more so than in the fields of knowledge. Certainly, specialization of knowledge provides advantages. It is inevitable as human knowledge grows deeper in any given science or in its technological applications, it requires increasing degrees of specialization. However, allowing and encouraging this specialization to exist completely separate, refusing to create necessary connections into other fields any given specialization impacts, has led to various and increasing dysfunctions for society as a whole.

Any specialized field shielded from larger context insures ineffectual politics. While specialization has reached historically unprecedented levels across society, the problems created by exclusivity are not new. Ober talks about how the Greeks countered specialization,

"Attention to the political foundation upon which the growth of human social capital was predicated helps to solve an apparent paradox: In classical Hellas the benefits of specialization were in such an abundance because specialization did not go 'all the way down' in the ways that are typical of centralized authority systems. Much of the work of governance in a democratic polis was done by amateurs—by citizen farmers and citizen-shoemakers, and citizen-soldiers who chose to dedicate themselves, part time to the tasks of rule-making, judgment, and administration."

With centralization of power, the amateur check on power is lost, creating ever greater concentrations of power through specialization. Ober shows the Greeks understood this peril. He writes,

"As Thucydides' Pericles had repeatedly pointed out, there would be no chance for Athenians to pursue private interests if the polis failed as a collective enterprise...if the educated elite used their near-monopoly as assembly speakers to warp debates in the direction of the interests of the wealthy and against those of ordinary citizens, the democracy would quickly unravel."

What better describes governance in the present United States? In the last decades, an educated, or more accurately, a badly educated elite have done nothing but warp political debate for their own and their wealthy patrons' interests. This was accomplished through the concentration of political, economic, and cultural power. Political power was gradually concentrated in Washington DC, where it is ludicrously maintained 535 people represent 350 million Americans.

What most detrimentally rose out of specialization is expert culture. With all of society sinking in an ocean of information, and ironically, simultaneously in ignorance, reliance for too many decisions is left exclusively to the specialists, that is the experts of any field, with an inability for greater society to judge either the specialists' aptitude or interests, which time and again prove lacking in the former and exceedingly greedy in the latter.

Again, none of this is new to the human experience, unprecedentedly massive in scale and determinative in structure? Absolutely! Ober writes of Athens,

> "Athenian citizens proved to be quite good at identifying and attending to experts and quite capable of using the knowledge of experts for the ends of policy-making without turning state management over to them. Plato, who was highly critical of democracy on many dimensions readily conceded the point in his dialogue, *Protagoras*. Plato noted that when for example, the assembly was discussing the construction of warships, the 'wise Athenians' listened only to the relevant experts; ignorant citizens who wasted the assembly's time with ill-informed opinions were quickly hooted from the speaker's platform."

Pretty much all running for office in America today should be hooted from the platform. Swapping faces is going to do absolutely nothing in solving the challenges America and indeed humanity face. The changes that need to come are not in personnel, but are systemic. Power needs a massive devolution.

Advantageously, the United States does have an extensive established infrastructure of county government. Essentially, the changes needed to be implemented are much more than governance, involving the larger political, economic, and cultural environments. However, distributed networking of county governments can create a foundation upon which the rest can be restructured.

There's three important components to be considered in restructuring. The first is making participatory organizations ubiquitous. Second, networking these entities into distributed ordered systems. And finally, an understanding at the heart of this organization lies the ability to create, edit, and enact the infinite mass of information created by contemporary knowledge and society.

Distributed organization at the county level immediately creates three important environments. First, in regards to the economy, such networks would quickly gain a unifying understanding of the restrictions imposed by current centralized economic powers. Secondly, in dealing with humanity's numerous existential environmental challenges, such networks gain the advantages of rebuilding around local ecologies and geographies. Finally, it fosters the creation of participatory structures, thus a rebuilding of reciprocity around citizen identity, requiring a revaluing of political and economic equality.

Bringing in a lesson from the Roman Republic, Western history's third great democratic experience, the great 19th century German historian Theodor Mommsen writes in his *History of Rome*,

> "The great principle established amidst severe conflicts, that all Roman citizens were equal in the eye of the law as respected rights and duties.... gradations to which differences of age, sagacity, cultivation, and wealth necessarily give rise in civil society, naturally also pervaded the sphere of public life; but the spirit animating the burgesses and the policy of the government uniformly operated so as to render these differences as little conspicuous as possible."

American culture once mixed patricians of wealth and the plebeians. Wealth itself was not so extraordinarily concentrated or conspicuous, most especially in public spaces, where wealth and everyone else often strode side by side. Maybe most exemplified by baseball stadiums, where today, wealth conspicuously gathers in so-called sky boxes. It is no coincidence sky-boxes were created by corporations. In ways, such separation is as detrimental and maybe more so than the knowledge hierarchies created by expert culture.

The great question is how to create more participatory organization. At this point, the only truly participatory governance in America is in the courts' jury system. The great jurist Louis Brandeis noted,

"...when I began to practice law I thought it awkward, stupid, and vulgar that a jury of twelve inexpert men should have the power to decide. I had the greatest respect for the judge. I trusted only expert opinion. Experience of life has made me democratic. I began to see that many things sanctioned by expert opinion and denounced by popular opinion were wrong."

Sapolsky notes on participation,

"A community with high levels of such participation is one where people feel efficacious, where institutions work transparently enough that people believe they can effect change. People who feel helpless don't join organizations."

As opposed to the democracies of Ancient Athens and the early American republic, these ideas and organization are lost to the United States of today. Our politics, hopelessly broken, remains focused on changing a few seats in Washington DC. A more and more desperate belief that somehow this will create a difference, even as each election cycle makes it clearer and clearer DC will not be fixed.

THOUGHTS ON DEMOCRACY

Here's three similar and important thoughts on democratic organization from three disparate figures across the 19th century.

"Where every man is a sharer in the direction of his ward-republic, or of some of the higher ones, and feels that he is a participator in the government of affairs not merely at an election, one day in the year, but every day; when there shall not be a man in the state who will not be a member of some one of its councils, great or small, he will let the heart be torn out of his body sooner than his power be wrested from him by a Caesar or a Bonaparte. As Cato then concluded every speech with the words *Carthago delenda est*, so do I every opinion with the injunction 'divide the counties into wards.'"

— THOMAS JEFFERSON, 1816

"Is there a man whose soul is so mean as to wish to depend on the whims of a single member of his community rather than to obey the laws he himself has helped to establish, that is if he thinks his nation exhibits the virtues necessary to make a proper use of liberty? I do not think such a man exists. Even despots accept the excellence of liberty. The simple truth is they wish to keep it for themselves and promote the idea that no one else is at all worthy of it. Thus, our opinion of liberty does not reveal our differences but the relative value which we place on our fellow man. We can state with conviction, therefore, that a man's support for absolute government is in direct proportion to the contempt he feels for his country."

— ALEXIS DE TOCQUEVILLE, 1845

"A Possible Future − Is it impossible for us to imagine a social state in which the criminal will publicly denounce himself and dictate his own punishment, **in the proud feeling that he is thus honoring the law which he himself has made, that he is exercising his power, the power of a lawmaker**, in thus punishing himself? He may offend for once, but by his own voluntary punishment he raises himself above his offense, and not only expiates it by his frankness, greatness, and calmness, but adds to it a public benefit."

— FRIEDRICH NIETZSCHE, 1881

None of our present institutions facilitate the participatory governance advocated by all three. Our politics are completely devoid of the notion of participation, at this point even in the barest sense of making educated choices. The politics of the 21st century require rethinking just to create meaning.

DEMOCRATIC AND ENVIRONMENTAL NECESSITY

"Accelerated change invokes the gyroscopic or principles of rigidity. Also, to high-speed change no adjustment is possible. We become spectators only, and must escape into understanding. This may be why the conservative has an advantage in such an age of speedy change and is frequently more radical in his suggestions and insights than the progressive who is trying to adjust. The practical progressive trying to make realistic adjustments to change exhausts himself in minor matters and has no energy to contemplate the overall."

— MARSHALL MCLUHAN, 1960

It's difficult to write about democracy. At this point, it's hard to claim there's any such thing. Thrown around by America's political class, it's pretty clear the term is close to meaningless. One remaining, unhelpful understanding of democracy, especially amongst certain segments of the population self-identified as liberals and progressives, is the idea of democracy as protest. Historically, there could be nothing further from the truth, today it mostly exemplifies the degradation of democratic thought.

Political protest signals there is no democracy or at best it's failing. Going back to democratic rule in Ancient Athens, for two-centuries there was little protest. How can there be protest when the citizenry is equally enfranchised in political decision making? If you lose a vote, you go back and work to change it. Who would you be protesting? Historically, assembled protest is a tool of the disenfranchised. The 1st Amendment's right to assembly is the democratic expression of a newly enfranchised citizenry emerging from the tradition of militarily imposed monarchical rule, not a democratic means.

The recent tradition of protest as democracy emerged from the 1960s cultural politics, a misinterpretation of the preceding Civil Rights Movement, where the descendants of America's slave caste successfully struggled for political enfranchisement denied to their ancestors and to themselves in the hundred years since abolition. Here protest was quite legitimate, not a political tool of democracy, but a necessity of the disenfranchised.

This was misunderstood by the following cultural movement, largely catalyzed by the societal bottom shaking of the Civil Rights Movement. It came to be believed protest was a great tool of democracy. Mostly ignored was the Civil Rights Movement truly determinative democratic organizing efforts, the greatest democratic organizational achievement in American, and it might be argued, global history. The movement's protest marches overshadowed the democratic tilling from which they sprouted. This is especially true in the media's coverage, which ignored the innumerable, decades long, face to face meetings in small churches and community rooms, where people were educated, organized, debated, deliberated, and made choices. This was the movement's democratic legacy.

In his seminal *I've Got the Light of Freedom,* Charles Payne writes,

"One of the persistent movement criticisms of the national press corps, the very idea of a 'national press corps' grew partly out of the movement, is that the press focused on big dramatic events while neglecting the processes that led to them."

As television destroyed and supplanted community and local political organization, gaining media attention became a main focus of most political action. Simultaneously, campaigns and elections became exclusively promoted as the only element of democracy. Lost completely was the essential understanding the real work of democracy is in education, face to face organizing, and group deliberation, all necessary if a vote is to be of any value.

The great deficiencies of protest politics become glaringly apparent with environmental issues. For Americans there are no great villains in environmental politics, not the oil companies, chemical companies, or Big Ag. The instigators are everyone, the collective daily actions of each American — no one is innocent, everyone a victim. Protesting against any given large, powerful entity misses the point, a scapegoating of responsibility for the every day combined actions of hundreds of millions. Definitive solutions will only be found changing those actions.

In Aeschylus' play *Prometheus Bound,* chained to his rock atop a cliff, Prometheus states, "Skill is weaker by far than necessity," an excellent encapsulation of the environmental challenges humanity faces. Necessity is the food, air, water, and shelter we require to live. With industrial technology, with skill, life's necessities were radically and in many cases detrimentally reshaped and altered. Key to any environmental politics is to refocus on necessity, how we as a species come by food, air, water, and shelter.

Wielding the power of necessity over skill, requires a revitalization of democracy, a political focus on the fundamental understanding of humanity as a social animal in which education, face to face organizing, deliberation, and action are the fundamental democratic necessities. It is here environmental solutions can be found and democracy revitalized.

THE GENERAL WELFARE

A number of diverse thinkers in the middle of the 20th century looked at specialization, the channeling of information into discrete categories, categories widely defined to include thought, professions, or institutions, as an increasing societal problem. Specialization presented increasing difficulties in determining how information, science, technology, might best be utilized in that now discarded, eternally nebulous Platonic notion of *kalos,* "the good," call it universal value as opposed to specific.

Long ago, Thomas Jefferson quipped everyone thought Plato profound because nobody knew what he was talking about, certainly notions of the good exemplify this. Jefferson's jab is especially amusing coming from someone who in America's founding document replaced Locke's right of property with the pursuit of happiness. A decade later, in the constitution's preamble, his fellow revolutionaries followed with a just as ambiguous thought about promoting the general welfare. All these terms convey some sense of societal wide, universal value.

In his 1951 work *Science and Humanism,* renowned physicist Erwin Schrodinger concisely framed the specialization problem,

"It seems plain and self-evident, yet it needs to be said the isolated knowledge obtained by a group of specialists in a narrow field has in itself no value whatsoever, but only in its synthesis with all the rest of knowledge and only inasmuch as it really contributes in this synthesis something toward answering the demand 'who are we?'"

He added,

"The awareness that specialization is not a virtue but an unavoidable evil is gaining ground, the awareness that all specialized research has real value only in the context of the integrated totality of knowledge."

Schrodinger declares as self-evident the problem of isolated knowledge in terms of the ancient Delphic Oracle's bidding to "know thyself," the finest example of paradox in the tradition of Delphi. For millennia, most especially in the last century America, this search for self-knowledge focused on some deeper nonexistent inner meaning, while the only possible answers are to be found in the world surrounding us, the world from which we came. Schrodinger's use of "who are we" as opposed to "know-thyself" is much more helpful. Who we are directly connotes the ability to understand the self by understanding we, that is the species *Homo sapiens*. Specialization does just the opposite, limiting understanding of ourselves with endless division, an inability to comprehend the "integrated totality of knowledge," that is the understanding of we, and thus an incapacity to promote the general welfare.

In 1951, Schrodinger was completely wrong thinking the awareness of specialization as an unavoidable evil was gaining ground. In fact specialization has become even more greatly championed, not just isolated knowledge, but domineering economic myths of the general welfare promoting individual greed. Each individual came to be defined by how they specifically fit into society, not by how their actions help define greater society. Foremost, individuals are now socially defined by how they "make a living," a process requiring ever greater specialization or as a comparably valueless, generic, eminently replaceable labor/service. In return, the individual defines themselves and greater society through acts of consumption. As Hannah Arendt in her sublime 1958 work *The Human Condition* astutely observed a society defined primarily by labor and its divisions "consumption takes the place of all truly relating activities."

Organization of society became more and more specialized, most especially with the corporation, which is inherently a specialist structure providing specific products or services. In regards to Schrodinger's integrated totality of knowledge, Plato's the good, Jefferson's pursuit of happiness, or the constitution's general welfare, today, all are exclusively and specifically measured as GDP. "It is not my business to cavil whether this mercantile attitude is moral or immoral, crass or subtle. It is my business to show that it leads to the misunderstanding and the mistreatment of information and its associated concepts." (Norbert Wiener, *The Human Use of Human Beings*)

Looking at how the ubiquity of specialized organization came to pass, we can begin with the great Scientific Revolution of the 16th and 17th centuries, a revolution that continues today. In a 1958 speech, atomic bomb creator J. Robert Oppenheimer talks about the development of specialized scientific knowledge,

"All these growths and wonder is almost unavailable to man in general. It is typically available in small specialized parts to rather small specialized groups, groups which it is true stretch from land to land, groups which feel across the physical frontiers and across the barriers of political and doctrinal hostility... but still small groups in marginal communication with each other and in marginal communication with man at large."

Today, it is simply impossible for any individual to have a great grasp of all the diverse generalities of science, while increasingly difficult for a specialist to just keep up with the growth of knowledge in their own individual field. As for Schrodinger's interest for a synthesis of specialization with the rest of knowledge, it is not even a concern. "The consequences for our ideas of education, our ideas of community and many of our political ideas are indeed not trivial." (Oppenheimer)

With growth in scientific knowledge comes ever more technology. Through technology, scientific understanding socially manifests itself, even if neither the ideas or the workings of the science or any given technology are understood beyond a small group of specialists. The questions of how any adopted technology then shapes the greater society are mostly ignored by the specialists and given less thought by society as a whole.

Having any ability to address the concerns and problems caused by the Scientific Revolution's unavoidable evil of specialization, compels us to dig even deeper to specialization's roots, particularly in how we as a species receive and process information. Looking from this perspective, our senses, the way we receive all information, are specialized, having specific implications. "Even in the sense organs there is a kind of organization, preorganization, of what it is you will learn of, of what it is you will notice, of what will be part of the structure of knowledge... the sense datum." (Oppenheimer)

The senses are specialized, data received as sound, touch, smell, taste, and sight. Specialized data of any sort automatically limits other data, "in a kind of precognitive way the cost of knowledge is a great deal of ignorance, the cost of perception is a great deal of imperceptiveness. ...one has to adopt the view that the potential is infinitely larger than the real." (Oppenheimer)

This is a perspective offered by a person responsible for one of history's most destructive technologies. Implementing and adopting any technology limits perception, creating ignorance of alternatives. The greater the societal adaption of the technology, the greater the limitations. Every technology defines our experience just as each sense. Once again, an easy example is the barely century old American car culture. Since inception, it has completely redesigned the American landscape to the point it becomes impossible for people to consider alternatives. Around for the same short period, the screen is proving both more powerfully socially transformative and limiting than the automobile. With technological adoption "over centuries by the rigorous separation and specialization of the senses," Marshall McLuhan wrote in *Understanding Media,* we become increasingly numbed to alternatives

It is imperative to understand both the extraordinary power of specialization and its resulting restrictions, whether it concerns knowledge, technology, or social organization. To use a contemporary political term, specialization results in prejudice. McLuhan writes, "Any specialist task leaves out most of our faculties." Society in the 21st century is a great jumble of specializations, some with much greater power than others. For example, Microsoft's power as a corporation compared to an independent software coder or most other Tech companies to constrict future development.

With technology development, we have no coming together, no synthesis or ability to view society as a whole — the general welfare — understood by the Greeks and America's founding generation as an inherent responsibility of politics. Our politics are completely broken, our institutions archaic, — government, corporate, and cultural — incapable in every way of synthesizing the whirlwinds of specialization we are engulfed.

MYCENAE AND THE EUMENIDES

Mycenae is a historic and legendary city of Greece. Inhabited since 5000 BC, its glory years spanned 1600 to 1100 BC. This late Bronze Age Mycenaean civilization stretched across the Greek mainland. Its influence on the Greek civilization that followed, between 800 and 400 BC, mostly a matter of conjecture. The great collapse of the Bronze Age civilizations of the Eastern Mediterranean, including

Mycenae, occurred 300 years before the origins of what we know as Classical Greece.

Mycenae is spectacularly perched on a hill above a fertile plain stretching across to the even more ancient city of Argos, just beyond Argos the "wine-dark" Aegean is visible. On the top of the hill sits the ruins of the small walled acropolis that served as a political center with a palace, temples, and fortress.

One thing we do know of these Bronze Age cultures, particularly Mycenaean and its immediate influential predecessor the Minoans centered on the island of Crete, politically, they were highly central-ized. Archaeologists define them as "palace cultures." The most impor-tant thing both civilizations bequeathed to Classical Greek's decentralized city-states was their collapse.

However, Mycenae holds an immensely important place in Ancient Greek mythology and culture. From Mycenae hails the great King Agamemnon. He united the Greeks to retrieve his brother's wife, the heavenly beauty Helen, who had sailed away with Paris and the Trojans. "And as for Troy, there she brought a dowry of destruction," Aeschylus ruefully notes of Helen's legacy. Of course this is the great story of the *Iliad*, attributed to Homer sometime from the 8th century BC, three centuries after the collapse of Mycenae.

An interesting thing about Greek mythology established by Homer is it continually evolves for another thousand years. For example, today, maybe the most popularly known element of Troy is the great wooden Trojan Horse, which never appeared in the *Iliad* and mentioned in only one line of the *Odyssey*. The story known today was largely fleshed out by the Roman, Virgil, eight centuries after Homer.

No era was more profound in shaping Homer's Greek mythology than that of the great tragedy and comedy playwrights of classical Athens, three or four centuries later. In *The Oresteia,* the great trage-dian Aeschylus uses Homer's story to directly tie legendary Mycenae to the founding of Athens' democratic courts and jury system. *The Oresteia* trilogy is named after their protagonist Orestes, Agamemnon's son. The main plot line first appeared in Homer's *Odyssey*.

Agamemnon is the first play. After spending ten years away fighting at Troy, the king returns to Mycenae accompanied by his Trojan captive and mistress, the haunted Cassandra, whose horrifying premonitions of the future of Troy and then her Greek conqueror prove all too true.

Agamemnon's wife, Clytemnestra, still has it against him that ten years before, in order to gain favorable winds for the Greek fleet to embark against Troy, at the behest of the goddess Artemis, he sacrificed their daughter Iphigenia. Phew, those Greeks! Incessantly harried by the immortal gods, though always their final fate directed by their own mortal hands. No sooner is he through the door then Clytmnestra and her lover Aegisthus murder Agamemnon and Cassandra.

In the second play, *The Libation Bearers,* Orestes, who was gone while his father was murdered, returns. In vengeance at the behest of the god Apollo, Orestes kills his mother and Aegisthus. Of course killing a parent is one of the ultimate sins of not just Greek but all human culture. For his crime, Orestes is bedeviled by the Furies, three goddesses representing vengeance and a certain crude justice. Orestes is driven mad and into the wilderness.

Here, we might ask ourselves, what would modern 20th century culture have looked like if instead of obscenely misinterpreting the actions of Oedipus, the quack Viennese doctor had chosen Orestes? No, we didn't want to bed our mothers, but kill them. Of course Oedipus had no idea the woman was his mother, but the disturbed Austrian sought to begat all sorts of secular incantations seeking to calm the modern Furies. Looking culturally at the 20th century, it would be hard to attribute anything more socially destructive or harmful than this misinterpretation of the Greeks creating a new and highly profitable school of myths, resulting in a culture of narcissistic self-absorption. One thing for certain, don't blame the Greeks.

In the third play, *The Eumenides,* it is clear we remain both beneficially and essentially indebted to the Greeks. From the wilderness, Orestes turns up at Delphi to appeal to the god Apollo, who had directed Orestes' revenge killing. Apollo, distressed at the Furies torment of Orestes, turns to the wisdom of the goddess Athena. She decides to hold a trial on the "Hill of Ares", which in Aeschylus' time was used for trials.

Athena states,

"Men of Attica, hear now my decree: You will be pronouncing judgement upon the first trial ever involving bloodshed. This court of judges will forever rule in the land of Aegeus (Athens)."

(It should be noted, judges today would more resemble jurors. Trails were all conducted and decided by an assembly of a segment or of all the citizenry.)

At the time Aeschylus wrote, democracy was brand new. He founded the jury trial with the gods. Aeschylus attributes to Athena the removal of the tradition of family and tribal blood revenge. In its place she creates a nonviolent civic process of the larger Athenian polis.

Athena declares,

"I now establish this court. Neither profit nor lust should violate it and it should remain an august guardian of the land, vigilantly defending those asleep, and quick to avenge. These then are my words uttered for the good of my citizens for all future. Now let every man stand, pick up his ballot, think of his oath and judge accordingly."

It is not simply the establishing of a court, but an assembly of the citizenry deciding by vote. Apollo then counsels the jurors before this first ever casting of votes,

"Friends, be sure to count the votes accurately. Be careful you don't make any mistakes because mistakes in judgment are followed by great disaster. One less vote destroys a house, another, saves it."

The vote is tied, thus Orestes was acquitted in this new political process, the first decision civilly addressing the most heinous crime of matricide. The *Oresteia's* celebration and honoring of democratic politics was first performed in front of the entire citizenry of Athens, during their biggest festival, the Dionysia. The play reinforces justice as the foundation of civil order. For the Greeks, justice was the essential political principle.

More ancient than Athena, the Furies are not happy. They represent the old family and tribal justice of vengeance. The eye for eye unending cycle of violence that disallows larger civil harmony. The Furies cry,

> "O gods! Gods of the younger generation! You've dishonored the old laws. You've snatched them from my own hands! And I, now with no honor, wretched and with anger heavily weighing on me shall spew upon this land the vindictive poison, the poison in my heart."

But Athena seeks to calm the Furies assuring them justice has indeed been accomplished. She pleads to the Furies the merits of this new process,

> "Listen to me! No injustice has been done and none suffered by you. I understand Justice and promise you that you shall have temples and lawful crypts in the land, to sit on bright thrones and altars and to be honored by these citizens."

Thus Aeschylus ends his play with a warning to honor justice and the democratic systems procuring it. Without them, the Furies will rule. In Ancient Athens, the mythical legends of Mycenae were sculpted into a very hard political reality.

Today, directly descended contemporary versions of democracy stretch across the planet. Standing at the top of the Hill of Ares, Athena needn't look hard to see her systems neither honored or producing much justice, assurances to calm the Furies of little avail.

EVOLVING DEMOCRACY: THE COURTS

> "It as long been my opinion, and I have never shrunk from its expression,... that the germ of dissolution of our Federal Government is in the constitution of the Federal Judiciary--an

irresponsible body (for impeachment is scarcely a scare-crow), working like gravity by night and by day, gaining a little today and a little tomorrow, and advancing its noiseless step like a thief over the field of jurisdiction until all shall be usurped from the States and the government be consolidated into one. To this I am opposed."

— THOMAS JEFFERSON, LETTER TO CHARLES HAMMOND, 1821

Ironically, Jefferson endures as one of the greatest critics of the American institutions he helped birth. His critiques almost always emanate from a democratic politics, in opposition to institutions taking power away from the greater population where power rightfully resided. Unbeknownst to Jefferson's legion of contemporary foes, across most of American history Jefferson was ostracized for his democratic thinking.

Little is remembered of Jefferson's warnings on the growing unchecked power of the federal courts. However, two-hundred years later, a contemporary Jeffersonian writes a little noticed book that includes an excellent chapter on the power of our now undemocratic and completely entrenched federal courts. Attorney Thomas Geoghegan's, *The History of Democracy Has Yet to Be Written* has an excellent critique of oligarchical governance by our federal courts. Geoghegan writes, "The federal courts do the governing of the world: intellectual property, labor, speech, police, race, corporate deals, everything, everything, and everything."

He polemically and beautifully indicts,

"The US Supreme Court distracts us from this real deep state; it even distracts many sensible pundits. It distracts us from the real way we are being governed. Watching the US Supreme Court as we do is like watching episodes of "The Crown," inasmuch as it helps anyone understand the real way the country is governed. It is a mistake just to focus on the court, or who is on it, just as it is a mistake to think that Washington, DC, exists only or even mostly within DC. The real Washington, DC, is just as much out here, in St. Louis or Phoenix or Miami, where the federal judges sit, as the real Roman Empire was in the provincial cities where its proconsuls were. Except under our form of government, these proconsuls serve for life, and we are not nearly as good as the Antonine emperors in keeping track of them. There may be quality control, of a kind, at the time of confirmation, but then that quality control stops for the next thirty or forty years."

"A quality control, of a kind" existing at all through the Congress is debatable. With a completely debauched and corrupted political system, quality of any sort has little or nothing to do with any of it. Tom adds, "All these lower federal courts collectively have far more power than the US Supreme Court or federal agencies—and if I could choose, I'd rather appoint all the district and appellate court judges in this country."

Geoghegan correctly looks at our archaic institutions of government, the system Jefferson and his cohorts bequeathed to us as the source of the problem. He writes,

> "While the judiciary may look like the weakest branch, and purports to defer to Congress, the entire lower bench as a body is much more capable at governing than the US House, which, thanks to the Senate, is often incapable of governing at all. In an antitrust case, a single federal judge can decide, as the US House cannot, how much power a company like Google can exercise over the land."

Beside the judiciary sits a modern priesthood, the attorneys, secularly ordained intermediaries between the citizenry and the courts. Remember a few years back, lawyers were the butt of jokes about unaccountable, shyster power. Then came 2008. Americans re-awoke to the bankers' filthy lucre, lawyers sort of faded into the background. Attorney Geoghegan reminds us,

"Yet who has even more power in our republic than all these lower court federal judges? We lawyers do. Because we lawyers decide what cases they are forced to hear. ...lawyers have incredible power to pull you in to have your deposition for three hours under oath; we have the power to make you recover from your hard drive all those documents you tried to delete the night before we sued you. If that is not a license to kill, it is at least a license to break and enter. It is the right—in a pretrial period that may last for years—to poke through your house, or your business, and ask what you have in that drawer, or over in that box, and while this poking around goes on for years, the judges who have the case may only check in occasionally to see what is going on."

Tom's democratic solution is inarguably a necessary restructuring of the federal system. He writes, "The court seems like an alternative to representative government, it's only because representative government, under our Constitution, is not a viable alternative in the first place."

Here, he correctly points to a major part of the problem – the Senate, "With too many vetoes, too many senators who, representing as few as 8 percent of the electorate, can stop a law." He calls for the Senate's abolition leaving the Congress as a single assembly, "If Congress were really the People's House, we would feel less need to pack the court, because the court would be less important."

Having with Tom, long ago advocated the abolition of the Senate, such reform is entirely too radical for our depraved political class to contemplate. Much more distressing, any real ideas of reform are completely absent from the collective or even the individual minds of the American people, who from birth are instilled with reverence for, though provided little understanding of, a constitution that today is used to politically disenfranchise them more than liberate.

It is the great political paradox of this era where the majority of Americans grow ever more alienated from their institutions, ideas for reforming them remain nonexistent. While Geoghegan is spot on identifying one important problem, his reform, though radical to many, remains nestled in the original government structure. A structure completely shaped by the Agrarian Era from which it sprouted, but then supplanted by industrialism, and now completely hapless in a burgeoning new technological era.

It is forgotten, except when convenient for various varieties of political Neanderthals, not that I have anything against Neanderthals though the best are long extinct, the constitution was originally (I used the word intentionally for our constitutional scholars) based on the literal uniting of the states. "In order to form a more perfect union" between the states, the constitution was unanimously ratified by the states. The constitution establishes the Senate as the states institutional power in the federal government. At the top of this piece, Jefferson laments the federal courts usurping the power of the states.

At the founding, all but the most zealous Federalists looked at the states as the greatest check and balance on federal power. In the newly formed District of Columbia, arguing about the states' power — "state's rights" — was prominent on many tongues, eventually growing everlastingly tarnished as the main constitutional defense of slavery.

Mr. Lincoln bloodily deconstructed this defense. After the decisive victory of Mr. Lincoln's bellicose argument, DC became unchecked sovereign. Over the decades following, the courts played a crucial role codifying DC's dominance, wielding the Interstate Commerce Clause along with various other imaginative interpretations of the constitution.

As representatives of the states, the Senate is basically an unneeded anachronism. From the beginning, a check on democracy, Geoghegan correctly defines today's Senate not as a check or balance, but a democratic obstruction. Today's Senate doesn't even represent the states, it is the ruling corporatocracy's greatest lever of power. Ridding DC of the Senate would certainly make the House more powerful. However, would it result in a more representative system? This is debatable, starting with the simple fact 435 people can in no way represent 350 million, not even considering the deplorable condition of the rest of the American political process.

A more constructive way to approach reform would be to turn our present way of looking at politics on its head, breaking the confines of our two-hundred and fifty year old governing architecture by restructuring from the ground up, using Jefferson's concept of self-government instituted through ward-republics as a guide. With regards to self-government, the essential questions are how decisions get made and who makes them. Geoghegan makes the incontrovertible case that decision making today is done largely by the federal courts, little about it democratic. A logical reform question follows, how can the courts be democratized?

With industrialization, the courts' role became increasingly defined by the accompanying massive growth of information. Today, information growth exponentially increases with the proliferation of new information technologies. Over a half-century ago, physicist and atomic bomb innovator, J. Robert Oppenheimer, astutely pointed to the problems facing governance from the exponential growth of science, technology, and the resultant explosion of information, stating,

"We face our new problems, created by the practical consequences of technology and the vast intellectual consequences of science itself, in a context of two or three billion people, in the context of an enormous society, in a context of a society for which none of our institutions were ever really designed."

If restructured, courts could play a healthy democratic role with the understanding the massive amount of information being produced to be democratically useful must be continuously edited, processed, and decided on. It is a role the present courts already play. They can be democratically restructured using an equivalent of the jury system, with the citizenry enfranchised to decide.

Doing this requires a restating and evolving the role of the citizen. Instead of the judges and attorneys, this role can be embraced by the citizenry. Just as today, the judge is expected to learn the general and particulars of each case, so too would jurors, randomly chosen for each case and compensated accordingly for time and effort.

The great Supreme Court Justice Louis Brandeis wrote,

"My early associations were such as to give me greater reverence than I now have for the things that are because they are. I recall that when I began to practice law I thought it awkward, stupid, and vulgar that a jury of twelve inexpert men should have the power to decide. I had the greatest respect for the judge. I trusted only expert opinion. Experience of life has made me democratic. I began to see that many things sanctioned by expert opinion and denounced by popular opinion were wrong."

This is a major problem for the 21st century, expert opinion may not simply be wrong, but entrenched in all sort of ways, processes, institutions, and maybe most detrimentally in simple habit, as opinion sheltered from alteration, whether by legislation, the courts, or public necessity. Every specialization creates its own priesthood, people with a deep understanding of a specific topic, issue, or entire school of thought, who deal only with each other, creating language only they understand.

Certainly this specialization, this division of intellect proved important, valuable, and necessary for the progress of science and technology. And there may be no way to particularly change this, there's a definite existential need for greater popular understanding and participatory judgment to foster a truly constructive and healthy politics for the 21st century and beyond.

Specialization proves especially detrimental in the question of how to utilize science's powerful offspring – technology. Specialization creates an environment where the technology becomes an unchecked power shaping the greater social, political, cultural and ecological environments. Without greater societal checks and balances, technology and technologists focus simply on what the technology can do, not whether it should be done or how it might best be done influenced by the greater environment. It is unnatural selection, a determining by part, not how it fits into the whole. Development of the technology becomes the end in itself. Outside their limited specialized knowledge, the scientist and technologist are no different from the rest of present society, detrimentally lacking a necessary larger view of the whole.

Restructuring the courts is not changing what they do, but helping enfranchise a larger view in the decision process. Courts do and in ways will always legislate. In an era of great change, our ideas about law need to change, especially in regards to technology and its impact on our lives. Law defined by technology is not that of the ancient tradition of Moses coming down from the mountaintop with stone tablets inscribed by flame for eternity. It is quite the opposite. It is many times very ephemeral rules made among ourselves for how things should work. We need much more organic processes of law, facilitating technological evolution with a constant shaping by the concerns and experience of the whole society.

Democracy is a corrective for these problems. Opening these issues and reforming decision making processes to ever greater numbers, in itself, brings a more representative perspective. This requires an evolving of democratic thinking, processes, and institutions, an acceptance of a Jeffersonian imperative each generation is rightfully endowed to revise and devise their own governance. An understanding, indeed an ethos, that the history of democracy has yet to be written.

IT'S ALL GREEK TO ME: *ANAXIMANDER AND THE BIRTH OF SCIENCE*

> If you keep these ideas in mind,
> You will easily see Nature is free:
> Liberated from her superb masters,
> She can do all things by herself
> Without any need of Gods.
>
> — LUCRETIUS, *DE RERUM NATURA*

Reading 20th century physicists can be a particularly enjoyable enterprise. Most, for example Einstein, Heisenberg, and Schrodinger, write the most clearly about their contributions to physics. An exception is Bohr, but that's directly connected to his writing style which is similar to thick, thick, thick 18th century German writers a la Kant, that's not to say Bohr as Kant before, didn't have some beautiful and profound thinking to convey.

I started reading the physicists when Ronald Reagan began waving nukes as part of a degenerate America *uber alles,* neo-patriotism. I dug into the science of the bomb. The best of those who helped unlock the quantum world had misgivings on the technologies being loosed by this knowledge. Another characteristic these physicists shared, they all had a great appreciation of the Ancient Greeks. It seemed ironic to find those who intellectually bequeathed the most powerful technologies of modernity appreciated the Greeks, especially at a time American universities found no use for the same thought of the ancient white boy slavers. "Ostracize the lot!" The cry echoed across the hallowed (or is it hollow) halls of academia.

I discovered a recent book by Italian physicist Carlo Rovelli, *Anaximander and the Birth of Science.* I hadn't previously been aware of Rovelli, who does quantum gravity research, but I never closely followed the last decades attempt of physics to unite general relativity and quantum mechanics. It all seemed a bit fantastical and beyond any ability to be experimentally verified. Certainly, relativity and quantum mechanics are in themselves fantastical in regards to accepted common sense, not just in how we traditionally think, but literally nonsensical in regards to the information we receive from our senses, nonetheless, to a certain extent both these theories have been experimentally and technologically proven.

Rovelli makes the case this scientific overturning of *Homo sapiens'* sensible understanding of the world began with the Greeks, particularly with Anaximander. It was Anaximander who first correctly conceived of the earth as suspended in space, resting on nothing. If you give it enough thought, this first scientific unmooring of daily experience remains as radical as any that followed.

Rovelli explains Anaximander, his teacher Thales, and the Greeks that followed were the initial developers of what's become known as the scientific method.

"Someone proposes an idea, an explanation. The process doesn't end there. The idea is seriously considered and criticized. Someone proposes a different idea, and comparisons are made. The extraordinary thing is that this process can converge toward agreement. In this way, a group of people can forge a common conviction, or a majority view, or in any event a shared decision."

Rovelli notes this method was specifically developed by the Greeks. He contrasts the Chinese, who for two thousand years had an imperial observatory tied to devising the calendar, but never developed an accurate measure of the earth. It wasn't provided until the Jesuits arrived in Beijing in the 17th century. Phew, how rich is the irony there? The Jesuits, Europe's, great, imperial church defilers of the Republican Renaissance, used the Greeks to help unravel Dynastic China.

From its beginnings, science continually upended previously established and variously codified understandings of the world. Its technological offspring entirely revolutionized human life. In his *Nature and the Greeks,* one of the developers of quantum mechanics, Erwin Schrodinger, reveals initial Greek thought still remains fundamental to many of today's scientific constructs. Most intriguingly, Schrodinger writes of Democritus' conception of the universe's fundamental structure of atoms and void (space). Yet, Schrodinger himself partook in the still not completely understood undermining of this basic dichotomy. Having not read Rovelli's work, but with an understanding of the general field, I'm sure he's written plenty about this intellectual predicament. The important point is many of the initial constructs and processes of Greek science remain very much part of today's science.

It is not just the scientific forms of the Greeks still defining much present thinking, but also Greek political forms. The most enjoyable part of the book is Rovelli's tying the development of science to the rise of Greek democracy. He notes the end of the Bronze Age collapse of the dominant centralized and hierarchical palace civilizations across the eastern Mediterranean created the open environment for the rise of the new, distributed Greek city states.

"The old absolute power of kings and priestly castes collapsed, and a new space opened up in which a new culture was born. Men learned to distrust a sovereign's absolute power and the priests' traditional wisdom. Something profoundly new was born in both the structure of society and humanity's quest for knowledge."

He continues,

"The birth of science and the birth of democracy, therefore, have a common foundation: the discovery of the usefulness of criticism and dialogue among equals. In criticizing his master Thales, Anaximander did nothing more than transport onto the plane of knowledge what was already common practice in the *agora*, the places of assembly, in Miletus: not accepting uncritically or reverently the divine or semi divine lord of the day, but instead criticizing the ideas of a citizen magistrate, not out of lack of respect, but on the shared conviction of that a better proposal can always be found. ...The birth of science and the birth of democracy, therefore, have a common foundation: the discovery of the usefulness of criticism and dialogue among equals."

As modern democracy degenerates, it is now established science seeking to create a new palace culture, literally incorporated in the industrial corporation. Just as distressing, a cult of science rises, including increasing pronouncements made with the sole intention of ending discussion, ending debate, the very processes essential to the scientific method. Maybe most representative of this tragic mix is the atrocity of some technology specialist, who has made a quick, Croesus fortune via archaic and decrepit market structures, continually spouting out idiocies on whatever topic they desire. Almost as bad as the inane ramblings of a given fool rising to the top of a corrupt and dysfunctional American political system. The real failure is the established system's growing inability to healthily confront either. The decline of democracy is as detrimental for healthy science as it is for a healthy politics.

The fundamental connection of geometry between the Greeks, science, and politics has been forgotten. Physics is geometry sketched by calculus. Euclid's initial axioms remain valid, but Einstein needed 19th century Lorentzian innovations to curve space-time. Geometry is also essential for political understanding, all power is geometric. Democracy's institutions and processes need to be horizontally and distributedly connected like the Greek city states as opposed to the vertical and centralized palace cultures that preceded them. With industrialization, political organization has become almost entirely centralized. Power is located overwhelmingly at the top of massive corporate pyramids. Essential to the decline of American republicanism has been the ever greater concentration of power in both the corporation and its DC handmaiden. Most recently, corporations use compute technology to further centralize power. The industry itself has become a palace culture, overwhelmingly controlled by a handful of corporations' network structure of massively centralized stored data centers, processed by increasingly centralized compute technology. However, it seems the energy required for such structure is a serious impediment to large scale adoption of this next generation of compute technology.

It is more than a bit ironic a relatively recent revolutionary idea of science, that order is gained from innumerable quantities distributedly connected across the "bottom" and not, using Lucretius' words, by masters ordaining order from the top, has had zero impact on contemporary political thinking. Instead, democracy is crushed from above, coinciding with a complete trashing and forgetting of the Greek experience.

Any ability to revive democracy requires not only a reforming of politics and government, but just as imperatively, the processes of science need reform, a renaissance in Greek understanding that the processes and methods of both are existentially entwined. Rovelli writes,

"Conceiving a democratic political structure means accepting the notion that the best ideas emerge from the discussion of the many and not from the authority of a single power. It means acknowledging that the public criticism can determine the best ideas, and that it is possible to debate and converge at reasonable conclusions. These are the very hypotheses that underlie science's search for knowledge."

He essentially adds,

"Taking this path requires faith in human beings, their being reasonable, and their honesty in searching for truth. This kind of faith in human beings is that of the luminous humanism of the Greek cities in the sixth century BCE at the root of extraordinary intellectual and cultural flowering of the following centuries, which continues to bear fruit in the contemporary world."

The world today is enmeshed in a centuries old scientific revolution. The resulting technologies ever more forcefully alter human life and the greater environment from where we were birthed. Science provides no blueprint for the future. It neither tells us what technologies to develop or the best way to utilize them. We have taken on the power of our old gods in the ability to manipulate nature, but the insight of the Greek educated Roman Lucretius that nature is liberated from any masters is true today as it was two thousand years ago. We are left, just as the Greeks, with democracy, as the best and at this point the only way to shape the future.

ATHENS: A HISTORY OF THE WORLD'S FIRST DEMOCRACY

Thomas Mitchell's *Athens: A History of the World's First Democracy* is a great work of classical history. It ranks with the Italian Ferrero's and the German Mommsen's histories of the Roman republic in quality, breadth, and political insight. Mitchell is a professor at Trinity College in Ireland. After decades of our scorched earth cultural revolution, you have to dig pretty deep in the ruins of "old Europe" for such an extraordinary find.

In his epilogue, Mitchell explains why Athens remains acutely relevant at the end of our era of progress. He outlines the growing failures of modern democracy, failures needing to be rectified for any democratic reform and revival. Mitchell writes, "Representative democracy in its modern guise seems to be gliding inexorably towards oligarchy" — it's not gliding towards, it's already there.

Oligarchy is one of the still useful political terms bequeathed to us by Ancient Greece. Simply, it is the rule of the few over the many. Mitchell essentially adds oligarchy is politics where "political influence means personal gain." For the Greeks, in opposition was democracy – the rule of the many. Democratic political influence means each and every citizen participates in shaping the greater public good. Mitchell writes,

"In the Funeral Oration, Pericles emphasized the motivating power of self-rule and the manner in which it inspired loyalty and moved people to act with greater courage and decisiveness in pursuing actions that they themselves had deliberated and decided. High participation and benefits that came with it were to prove an enduring source of the stability and capability of the democracy."

Mitchell then rightfully indicts the present,

"But the Athenian achievement also has lessons for modern developed democracies, which have increasingly eroded the role of the people and are now pale shadows of the Athenian concept of government by the people."

There are numerous reasons for this disenfranchisement of the people from modern democracy, the greatest cause being the destruction of all politics except electoral politics. Elections are the essential final decision-making step of a healthy democratic system, not the only one. Today, the rest of politics no longer exists. "The trend of modern political thought and practice is to confine the role of the people to the electoral function. Schumpeter (Austrian economist) called it the 'rule of the politicians', not of the people." Mitchell continues, "But even the electoral role has been diluted and tarnished by the failure of modern democracies to create fair electoral processes."

The American election system has been compromised in all sorts of way. Most detrimental by defining democracy exclusively through campaigns as campaigns became defined by the methods and practices of industrial business. There is nothing democratic about marketing and advertising, polls and thirty-seconds ads, mass phonebanks and mailers, or over the last half-century, the professionalization of campaigns as they became just another business, a very lucrative business for a few.

As campaigns became a business, their defining medium became money. Mitchell writes,

> "US Supreme Court, which held that it is not an acceptable governmental objective 'to level electoral opportunities or equalize the financial resources of the candidates.' The Court considered that a limitation on campaign spending would constitute and infringement of freedom of speech. This is a far cry from the Athenian determination to root out corruption and forestall the possibility of any power group being able to control or manipulate the decision-making of government. It opens the door to the rule of money, the antithesis of all that democracy represents."

Bloomberg reports the 2022 U.S. election saw $17 billion spent. The excellent organization Open Secrets shows less than 1% of Americans contributed all this money, 0.48% contributed 75% of it, and 10 individuals alone placed over $1.2 billion into federal elections over the last decade. The elections' process is bought and sold a billion times over before any votes are counted. If this isn't oligarchy, I don't know what is.

This has led to a completely and entirely unaccountable system.

The foundation of Athenian democracy, every American founder understood this, was holding power accountable. Mitchell writes,

> "Another notable feature of the democracy that contributed to unity and stability was its diligence in protecting against two of the most insidious threats to good government: corruption and factionalism. The rigour of its system of accountability for all entrusted with public office left little scope for malfeasance or corrupt behaviour."

He adds,

> "When the Athenian demos delegated power to office-holders, that power came with a rigorous regime of accountability for its use. In modern democracies, where the power to rule is delegated in its entirety, there is no such regime. The electorate can replace those who no longer command its favour at the next election, but the prospect of losing one's seat is feeble safeguard against bad government or abuse of power."

In American politics reelection rates are well over 90%. In the starkest contrast, offices of all Athens' magistrates were held for only a year, with no ability to be chosen for another year. And at the end of their annual term, there was a rigorous accounting of each magistrate's actions with the ability to sanction the actions of all persons who had held any office. Accountability of any and all office-holders was the foremost democratic function. In America today, power is completely unaccountable.

Another great deficiency in today's politics, the heart and soul of any democracy, is the ability to have healthy discussions and constructive deliberations. The overwhelming majority of Americans have zero role in setting any political agenda or defining solutions. Mitchell writes of the present condition,

> "The concept of democracy, however, still retains its allure, but it is difficult to see how it can sustain its claim to be the system

that ensures the government of a state is carried out in line with the wishes of the majority of the people unless the people have a more meaningful role in debating and shaping the significant decisions that will deeply affect their lives... It can mean more than skeletal electoral democracy."

Adding,

"The pride in citizenship, the public spirited communitarian ethos, the sense of having a real say in directing the public good – characteristics that gave Athens its social cohesion and unprecedented levels of political government – are all becoming casualties of modern disempowerment."

Americans have no sense of ownership of politics. Their ability to direct the public good exists not at all. The political agenda is set by the political class and the corporate media. Social cohesion frays as factional predatory oligarchy creates division keeping the majority powerless.

Democracy is also a distributed information and communication system. In the past century, information and communication technologies have undergone the greatest revolution in human history. Democracy has lost out across the board. Any equivalents of the Ancient Athenian agora, assembly, council, juries, and the demes, where the citizenry interacted, learned, discussed, and debated, exist not at all, or are so dysfunctional they may as well not exist.

Mitchell correctly points to the deteriorated role of the established press. At America's founding, a free, massively distributed press both helped shape the political agenda and held officials accountable, today regarding the latter, the press holds no one accountable, while of the former, the media overwhelmingly advocate gross private interests. He writes,

"A vigorous free press is potentially an important arm of healthy democracy...providing a continuous flow of accurate information... duty to hold the government account, to subject the performance of government to rigorous scrutiny and to investigate any evidence of irregularity or corruption."

Then correctly diagnoses the current dilemma,

"But in many respects the mass media are failing the public...shifting from informing to entertaining...concentration of significant news organization in fewer hands leading to powerful media conglomerates that have dangerous levels of political leverage."

Our corporate media is overwhelmingly a propaganda tool of oligarchic control. A process developed over the last century with the growth in power of the industrial corporation and the development of broadcast mass media.

On the development of mass and digital media, Mitchell's view is unfortunately conventional:

"When it comes to the availability of knowledge of current political issues and challenges, modern society has an advantage over Athenians. The rise of mass media, and especially digital media, had led to a knowledge revolution, and a vastly easier and wider access to information."

This view has been accepted in the last couple decades especially in regards to the internet. At this point it's plain to see without radically restructuring the technology and just as essentially the human organization around it, these ideas are nothing but a false premise. Instead of bringing together for democratic politics, information technology increasingly fosters greater separation, an endless feeding of established prejudice, ignorance, and misinformation, no matter the professed political identity.

Quantity of information in no way represents quality. In the biggest contrast to Athens, today, the ability for any individual to utilize, in any healthy effective way, the mass of information they encounter over a given day is an impossibility. Creating the structure and processes, collective associations to edit this information is the single greatest organizational challenge of any democratic revival. It is not a new concern, the technology however is without precedent.

Mitchell again states accepted conventional wisdom, "In modern society more of that knowledge will have to come through the educational system. Preparing young people for responsible citizenship should be a goal of education at every level." There are two problems with this: first, the complete inadequacy of our entire contemporary education system; second, all that we now accept as an educational system is inadequate to meet the now life-long process of learning and interacting with an information rich environment.

Mitchell continues more helpfully,

"The ethos of civic engagement should be fostered by all the organs of state and by early involvement in local community activities. Athenian democracy drew strength from the vibrant community life of the demes."

The 139 Athenian demes were the local political/government organizations much ignored by historians. The biggest reason for this absence is the happenings and decisions of the demes were little recorded. These were the daily participatory processes where politics were conducted; deliberations, choices by lot to send people up to the Council that set the agenda for the greater citizen Assembly, and similarly provide candidates for all magistrate offices. The demes laid the foundation for the education, communication, and decision making of Athenian democracy. Up from the demes came the much better documented debates and decisions of the greater Athenian Assembly.

The demes are a model for how any future democracy would look. In the 21st century such organizations, call them associations, first and foremost concern would be the creation, editing and communication of information. They would be participatory and distributedly, not centrally, networked. One of the greatest insights of the last century of science is the still developing understanding of distributed network order. It is a most revolutionary organizational idea.

Any future democracy necessitates recreating democratic politics, most importantly, creating participatory structures that allow each and every citizen involvement in the processes of issue deliberation and meaningful participation in shaping resulting actions.

A half-century ago, the historically essential and classically learned democratic thinker Hannah Arendt pointed out one of the original sins of the American system was the failure to institute participatory processes and organization. Arendt understood the original democratic organizational structures of revolutionary America were the multitude of town halls spread across the colonial landscape. In *On Revolution*, she sublimely writes of America's great democratic failing,

> "It was precisely because of the enormous weight of the Consti-
> tution and of the experiences in founding a new body politic
> that the failure to incorporate the townships and the townhall
> meetings, the original springs of all political activity in the
> country, amounted to a death sentence for them. Paradoxical as
> it may sound, it was in fact under the impact of the Revolution
> that the revolutionary spirit in America began to wither away,
> and it was the Constitution itself, this greatest achievement of
> the American people, which eventually cheated them of their
> proudest possession."

She adds, "The Constitution itself provided a public space only for the representatives of the people, and not for the people themselves."

This was not unknown to the founders. Benjamin Rush of Pennsylvania stated, "All power is derived from the people, they possess it only on the days of their elections. After this it is the property of their rulers." With the capture and corruption of today's elections process, the people no longer hold power even on those days.

Any thinking on the revival of democracy requires a rethinking of politics itself, the word has become so degraded most consider anything political an insult. If you look at many elected officials it is. Politics, as Aristotle correctly noted, is the very foundation of what it is to be human. Like breathing, it is part of us all and largely, equally distributed. Mitchell astutely writes,

"Political judgement and wisdom are elusive qualities. They undoubtedly require a base of knowledge and experience but are mostly gifts of nature. Good judgement, being able to see the right course – what Thucydides called *gnome,* and considered the special attribute of Pericles – though it certainly needs a level of political knowledge, is not a necessary consequence of advanced education or any form of specialized learning. Great intellectuals do not necessarily make great politicians. It is not possible to say that political wisdom is the preserve of any social class or group of specialists. It is a quality that, to an extent, is within the grasp of everyone."

These observations I discovered fairly quickly in my political experience. A more learned, quicker intellect in no way represents political ability. Indeed, it's simply amazing how often a person most would consider smart was a political knucklehead. At the same time, I experienced innumerable occasions where people, most wouldn't consider in any way exceptional, offer astute and cutting political analysis.

Arendt wrote of the party system that had developed by the mid-20th century in America and all other modern republics, "It is in mature party systems that the authentically political talents can assert themselves only in rare cases." Today in America's political brand system, politics is tragically devoid of political talent.

Across my life, I've met or observed only a handful of truly exceptional political talents. Few enough that I concluded long ago it would be impossible to devise a system better than democracy for these and all people's political talents to best be realized. The greatest quality shared by all political talents I've met or observed is they seek the opinions of others, across the widest spectrum possible. This is the fundamental nature of democracy. Recently, in ahistorical Tech circles, a supposedly innovative understanding promoted as the wisdom of crowds appeared. It is in truth the most ancient political wisdom. Mitchell writes,

"Even Aristotle, a great thinker but no great admirer of democracy, conceded that political wisdom was not the exclusive preserve of an elite, and that a plausible argument could be made for popular rule. He made it in his so-called summation theory, which held that, while each individual within the mass (*hoi polloi*) may not have superior excellence, everyone has a share in goodness and practical wisdom (*phronesis*), and can contribute something, and the sum of these contributions makes the collective judgement of the many more likely to be right than that of the more expert few."

This is in diametric opposition to our specialized intellectual culture's celebration of experts as always providing the greatest insight. It is an unsophisticated faith in the judgement of established authority and in this era of rapid technology innovation simple know-how providing the best or even correct guidance in deciding if gained knowledge should be implemented, and if so, how.

We have a lot to relearn from Athens. Mitchell's book, like the still visible speakers' rostrum on the Pnyx of Athens, stands as reminder something valuable and unique was innovated here. It reminds us oligarchy is not new, similar situations have been faced across history and in response to one instance, democracy first arose. Mitchell concludes his history of the world's first democracy,

"It did go from the unequal, divided world of Solon, ruled by an entrenched, oppressive, faction ridden elite, to a society governed by an agreed code of law, which recognized the equal intrinsic worth of every citizen, and the rights of every citizen to an equal voice in deciding the public good. Athens remains a striking and valuable example of how a socially divided, unstable oligarchic society can radically transform itself and live by new values of freedom and equality and popular government under a strictly enforced rule of law."

✸ 3 ✸
THE POLITICS OF TECHNOLOGY

MOSAIC: WIENER, MCLUHAN, & THE POLITICS OF TECHNOLOGY

Note: I have pulled thinking from Wiener's and McLuhan's two works – The Human Use of Human Beings and Understanding Media respectively – attempting to combine the similarity of their thought as a basis for what can be considered a politics of technology. The similarities are quite striking and valuable, somewhat fascinating coming from their different perspectives. Where appropriate I've added various thoughts I've had over the years.

The writing is set up in sections and blocks of thought, aphorisms in certain respects, not meant as traditional narrative, but more as a mosaic, distinct pieces coming together to form a pattern or picture. It is meant in the words of Wiener not as know-how, but know-what, an attempt to provoke thought and invite the participation of the reader for full definition.

The quotes come from either McLuhan's *Understanding Media* – (Mc), Wiener's *The Human Use of Human Beings* – (W), or *Cybernetics* – (W Cy).

෪

Wiener and McLuhan

In his seminal 1964 work *Understanding Media: The Extensions of Man,* Marshall McLuhan notes a speech given by Radio Corporation of America Chairman of the Board David Sarnoff where he states, "We are too prone to make technological instruments the scapegoats for the sins of those who wield them. The products of modern science are not in themselves good or bad; it is the way they are used that determines their value." What's fascinating about this statement is its given by the head of one of the 20th century's great technology companies and it is completely wrong, but it remains the dominant belief of technologists, tech corporations, and most people today.

McLuhan wrote his book in direct opposition to this thinking.

"Technological media are staples or natural resources, exactly as are coal and cotton and oil. Anybody will concede that a society whose economy is dependent upon one or two major staples like cotton, or grain, or lumber, or fish, or cattle is going to have some obvious social patterns of organization as a result." (Mc)

Yet, as Sarnoff ignorantly and illustriously demonstrated, such thinking was and remains completely lacking. Instead, it is believed technologies are simply tools for shaping the larger environment, not environments in and of themselves.

"To the student of media, it is difficult to explain the human indifference to social effects of these radical forces. ...So extraordinary is this unawareness that it is what needs to be explained. The transforming power of media is easy to explain, but the ignoring of this power is not at all easy to explain." (Mc)

"Political scientists have been quite unaware of the effects of media anywhere at any time, simply because nobody has been willing to study the personal and social effects of media apart from their 'content'." (Mc)

Fourteen years before *Understanding Media,* the great math-ematician and scientist Norbert Wiener wrote an even more seminal work on technology titled, *Cybernetics: Or Control and Communication in the Animal and Machine.* Two years later, he produced a less mathemat-ical work on the same subjects, *The Human Use of Human Beings.* While McLuhan's included a deeper historical view of technology, Wiener focused more on the impact of the then new and developing compute, information, and communication technologies, though he also had a strong historical perspective. Wiener wrote of the new technologies,

> "I have been occupied for many years with problems of commu-nication engineering. These have led to the design and investi-gation of various sorts of communication machines, some of which have shown an uncanny ability to simulate human behav-ior, and thereby to throw light on the possible nature of human behavior. They have even shown the existence of a tremendous possibility of replacing human behavior, in many cases in which the human being is relatively slow and ineffective. We are thus in an immediate need of discussing the powers of these machines as they impinge on the human being, and the conse-quences of this new and fundamental revolution in technique." (W)

Unlike Sarnoff, Wiener and McLuhan understood technologies themselves, not just their content, have social and political implica-tions inherent in their very natures, requiring forethought in their implementation, and, importantly, continual reassessment using the "feedback" received from their implementation. The difference between McLuhan's and Wiener's understanding and Sarnoff's is best summed-up by Wiener, "There is one quality more important than know-how and we cannot accuse the United States of any undue amount of it. This is 'know-what': by which we determine not only how to accomplish our purposes, but what our purposes are to be." Know-how is engineering, the exclusive factor in the historical devel-opment of technology, something America has been profoundly adept.

Know-what is the politics of technology and America is completely bereft.

Technology and its adoption implements organization and values regardless of content, shaping culture, politics, and society as a whole. This politics has largely been missed or dismissed from our historical understanding, despite two-centuries of industrial technology radically altering human existence. Now, compute technologies promise even more radical change to society as a whole.

Without a politics of technology, technological development continues to be measured either with existing values, most deter-minedly and detrimentally those of profit, and increasingly the values of the technology themselves. Any politics of technology's funda-mental principle would be "the machines are secondary in all matters of value that concern us to the proper evaluation of human beings for their own sake and to their employment as human beings, and not as second-rate surrogates for possible machines of the future." (W)

McLuhan was a Canadian literature professor, who luckily or smartly, was little impacted in any way by the drivel theory that came out of many 20th century literature departments across Europe and America. It might not be so odd in that McLuhan looked at the devel-opment of the phonetic alphabet and millennia later the development of the printing press, regardless of their content, as two of the greatest technologies shaping world history. McLuhan was the greater historian, with his knowledge of literature helping offer wonderful expositions on technology's impact.

Wiener was a quintessential, if time now reveals disappearing American democrat, a mathematician, scientist, and engineer. These three fields greatly shaped his perspective. Wiener also had a back-ground in both history and literature, both proved invaluable in shaping his perspective. However, it was the science of 20th century physics, the most revolutionary since Newton's three centuries before, that greatly shaped his thinking, providing an integral understanding of developing compute and information technologies.

If there is a great difference between the two, it would be McLuhan's view of all technology as an extension of the human body. In this literal sense, technology defines how we physically and mentally interact with the world. Most significantly, *Homo sapiens* experienced all technology through the body's established sensory architecture, whether sight, hearing, touch, smell, or taste. The senses are how we receive information. In this thinking, McLuhan at times can be most confusing, at other times most wrong, and at times most valuable. Even today, our understanding of how our minds actually receive and process sensory information remains, let's say, primitive, if understood at all. Yet, McLuhan's thinking in this regard remains valuable and original. His very complex thinking about the screen and how we interact with it still deserves greater thought. The screen's entrancement, its staring into the fire quality, remains not well understood. Again, a big part of this is our still limited understanding on how the brain actually functions, but it is completely obvious from its inception the screen has proved infinitely captivating and addictive no matter its content. For what precise reasons might still not be understood, but no one can doubt the affliction.

Wiener deals with the human organism's and machine's interaction more indirectly, though with complete understanding of the machine as a mimic of human action and its growing ability to mimic human thought. Both understood technology redefines not simply human relations with the machine, but human relations between each other. The ability for humanity to come to terms with this power was in its very essence politics.

Communication and Information

In defining the species *Homo sapiens*, the greatest characteristic setting us apart might be our hyper-communication traits. Communication implies the transference of information, thus in talking about communication you are by definition talking about information. The definition of information has always been rather nebulous. With the growth of information technologies over the last three-quarters of a century, information has been predominately conceived statistically. With his groundbreaking theory on information, Claude Shannon paradoxically explained his definition had nothing to do with meaning, that is content.

"The concept of information developed in this theory at first seems disappointing and bizarre - disappointing because it has nothing to do with meaning, and bizarre because it deals not with a single message but rather with the statistical character of a whole ensemble of messages, bizarre also because in these statistical terms the two words information and uncertainty find themselves to be partners."

If you're dissatisfied with this definition remember the entire compute and communication industry has been built on it.

Human vocabulary is remarkably generalized and can be extremely nebulous, an inherent characteristic of our communication. As J. Robert Oppenheimer explained, our communications in everyday life are highly ambiguous. It is only with science and technological development a certain stringency becomes necessity. With ambiguity, or maybe better generality, comes a certain subjectivity and imprecision, yet human verbal communication is amazingly powerful, creating and holding together an almost infinite number of complex social networks.

Since the invention of the printing press five centuries ago, the processes of communication and the sheer quantity of information have risen exponentially. In the last century, both increased more rapidly with the rise of electric and then compute technologies.

"The needs and the complexity of modern life make greater demands on this process of information than ever before, and our press, our museums, our scientific laboratories, our universities, our libraries and textbooks, have been developed to meet the needs of this process. To live effectively is to live with adequate information." (W)

Today, adequate information is not simply necessary to live effectively, but to live at all, with human produced information increasingly incorporated into and shaping every aspect of life.

Largely imperceptible, information technology brings a content analogy of Shannon's definition of information as a statistical value into measure for each individual. As a daily information tsunami washes across each person, unnecessary information is "noise" surrounding "signals" of specific value, though this value may as likely be instilled as opposed to sought.

> "Ads seem to work on the very advanced principle that a small pellet or pattern in a noisy, redundant barrage of repetition will gradually assert itself. Ads push the principle of noise all the way to the plateau of persuasion. They are quite in accord with the procedures of brain-washing. This depth principle of onslaught on the unconscious may be the reason why." (Mc)

Organization has always played a fundamental role in valuing information. Both state and church have long asserted great power in valuing information, primarily by controlling various media of communication even if it was simply promoting or censoring specific words. "Those who have made the clear maintenance of the channels of communication their business are those who have most to do with the continued existence or the fall of our civilization." (W) Today, the business of communication is largely that, a business.

Overwhelmingly it is the mega-corporation who control the media of communication and assert specific value. The "communicative integrity of man I find to be violated and crippled by the present tendency to huddle together according to a comprehensive prearranged plan, which is handed to us from above. We must cease to kiss the whip that lashes us." (W)

The whip Wiener metaphorically notes is presently electronic communication, electric media having redefined the channels of communication and thus information.

> "Nowadays, with computers and electric programming, the means of storing and moving information become less and less visual and mechanical, while increasingly integral and organic. The total field created by the instantaneous electric forms cannot be visualized any more than the velocities of electronic particles can be visualized. The instantaneous creates an inter-

play among time and space and human occupations, for which the older forms of currency exchange become increasingly inadequate." (Mc)

McLuhan notes two interesting phenomena; first, electric speed decreases the value of stored information. "The idea that information can be stored in a changing world without an overwhelming depreciation in its value is false. ...information is even more a matter of process than a matter of storage." (W) Secondly, information increasingly defines every activity, every process, in so doing, established methods of valuing information via separate media, "forms of currency exchange," money being both the easiest and powerful example, become increasingly incapable of providing meaningful value. Money evolved in an era of less information. Its value derived by providing a simple numerical, quantitative worth to all information. Much information is devalued in this process. The massive increase in debt across the economic system correlated with the ever greater adoption of electronic compute and communication technology is symptomatic of this process. At this point we haven't the social means of directly valuing most information without first assigning it a monetary value. At the same time, the entire political structure is largely built on this value system and its preservation. Reform to incorporate more direct values, an appreciation of the value of process, requires not new technologies, but new human associations.

Linear and Mosaic

Technology creates its own environment. The use of any technology employs a certain perspective of the world. As any technology becomes ubiquitously adopted, its perspective can become so dominant people have a difficult time discerning the world outside this specific perspective. A technology can come to be seen as natural or as necessary as water to human life. In the US, the easiest example is the automobile, which has so altered the physical landscape, it has come to define the individual, making it logical for most to consider life without an automobile an impossibility as a fish would consider water.

The automobile is a relatively recent technology. However, technology's shaping of human perspective reaches far back across the human story. One defining perspective provided by technological development, though little conceived of as technology has been the phonetic alphabet. There's a number of powerful perspectives provided by the phonetic alphabet and writing, most important is the ability to define and think linearly.

"The visual stress on continuity, uniformity, and connectedness, as it derives from literacy, confronts us with the great technological means of implementing continuity and linearity by fragmented repetition. The ancient world found this means in the brick, whether for wall or road. The repetitive, uniform brick, indispensable agent of road and wall, of cities and empires, is an extension, via letters, of the visual sense." (Mc)

At this point, the idea of linear thinking is so culturally embedded, it is almost impossible to imagine it was fostered by the phonetic alphabet and literacy.

"Literacy is indispensable for habits of uniformity at all times and places. Above all, it is needed for the workability of price systems and markets."(Mc) That these developments derived from the technology of the phonetic alphabet and literacy are rarely considered. Yet, in the last century, with the development of electric media and particularly the screen, literacy as a dominant medium for communication is increasingly challenged along with linearity as the governing organizational scheme. "This factor has been ignored exactly as TV is now being ignored, for TV fosters many preferences that are quite at variance with literate uniformity and repeatability." (Mc)

This was McLuhan's greatest insight, the challenge to the dominance of literacy and linear thinking by electricity and the screen. He deduced perspective created by electricity as not linear, – where B follows A and C follows B – but more of a mosaic, where perspective comes simultaneously from A, B, and C. Just as important, the receiver is not passive, but a participant in shaping the pattern received. "The plunge into depth experience via the TV image can only be explained in terms of the differences between visual and mosaic space. Ability to discriminate between these radically different forms is quite rare in our Western world." (Mc)

Today, the screen is connected across the planet receiving and sending instantaneous information and perspectives from which, tactility, the receiver is completely removed.

"Our highly literate societies are at a loss as they encounter the new structures of opinion and feeling that result from instant and global information. They are still in the grip of "points of view" and of habits of dealing with things one at a time. Such habits are quite crippling in any electric structure of information movement, yet they could be controlled if we recognized whence they had been acquired. But literate society thinks of its artificial visual bias as a thing natural and innate." (Mc)

In general, McLuhan is absolutely correct in understanding this fundamental shift in perspective. One can certainly argue, and should, about what it means. Sixty years on, the screen has become more ubiquitous, instantaneous, and for all intents and purposes, infinite in communication and information quantity. We have little understanding how this technology is shaping us both as individuals and society, most especially as we've historically disregarded technology's shaping force. Literacy and linearity are still foundational to the organization of society and essential to the creation of technology. Yet as a means of communication, literacy is becoming ever more specialized, irrelevant in many ways to shaping the greater social whole where the mosaic created by the networked screen increasingly dominates. "Scarcely a single area of established relationships, from home and church to school and market, has not been profoundly disturbed in its pattern and texture." (Mc)

Paradoxically, if events continue as currently established, literacy will once again become largely a tool of a small elite just as it was before the printing press. An elite using the tool of literacy to shape and control technology, the environment of the electric mosaic, through which the vast majority communicate and interact.

Feedback

In an electric system with the ability to send and receive instantaneous messages simultaneously from numerous sources, linear organization becomes problematic. Linearity is even more greatly challenged when an electric system incorporates feedback.

"Anybody who begins to examine the pattern of automation finds that perfecting the individual machine by making it automatic involves 'feedback.' That means introducing an information loop or circuit, where before there had been merely a one way flow or mechanical sequence." (Mc)

Wiener was essential in developing the idea of feedback, defined as, "For any machine subject to a varied external environment, in order to act effectively it is necessary that information concerning the results of its own action be furnished to it as part of the information on which it must continue to act." (W)

In *Cybernetics,* Wiener notes,

"The first significant paper on feedback mechanisms is an article on governors, which was published by Clerk Maxwell in 1868, and that governor is derived from a Latin corruption of $\chi\upsilon\beta\varepsilon\rho\nu\acute{\eta}\tau\eta\varsigma$ (cybernetic). We also wish to refer to the fact that the steering engines of a ship are indeed one of the earliest and best-developed forms of feedback mechanisms."

Wiener's understanding was seminal in understanding what feedback would mean for electric and compute technologies.

The process of feedback complicates the linearity of industrial development, fostering the creation of the non-linear information technology mosaic.

"Feedback is the end of the lineality that came into the Western world with the alphabet and the continuous forms of Euclidean space. Feedback or dialogue between the mechanism and its environment brings a further weaving of individual machines into a galaxy of such machines throughout the entire plant. There follows a still further weaving of individual plants and factories into the entire industrial matrix of materials and services of a culture. Naturally, this last stage encounters the entire world of policy, since to deal with the whole industrial complex as an organic system affects employment, security, education, and polities, demanding full understanding in advance of coming structural change. There is no room for witless assumptions and subliminal factors in such electrical and instant organizations." (Mc)

"It is certainly true that the social system is an organization like the individual, that it is bound together by a system of communication, and that it has a dynamics in which circular processes of a feedback nature play an important part. ....This complex of behavior is ignored by the average man, and in particular does not play the role that it should in our habitual analysis of society." (W Cy)

This is a terribly important and relative point for our era. Our associations — social organization, corporations, and government — are all overwhelmingly one directionally linear. This is not coincidence, most social order has roots deep in linear text organization back to the founding of the phonetic alphabet. Reforming societal associations to not simply accept feedback, but be shaped by it, is the most fundamental political reform of the 21st century.

Of course, the question of designing feedback into social systems today immediately raises the question of incorporating the machine. In understanding the roles of the machine in this sense, we need to understand the process of feedback in machine automation. Wiener writes of the compute machine in 1950,

"For a large range of computational work, they have shown themselves vastly more rapid and vastly more accurate than the human computer. Their speed has long since reached such a level that any intermediate human intervention in their work is out of the question. Thus they offer the same need to replace human capacities by machine capacities as those which we found in the anti-aircraft computer. The parts of the machine must speak to one another through an appropriate language, without speaking to any person or listening to any person, except in the terminal and initial stages of the process. Here again we have an element which has contributed to the general acceptance of the extension to machines of the idea of communication." (W)

In the 75 years since, this process increased exponentially. Compute technology has become ever more ubiquitous in every aspect of society. The technology ever more proficient in communicating with itself. Wiener understood very well and profoundly cautioned against simplistically thinking of the machine removing the human element as automatically advantageous:

"Any machine constructed for the purpose of making decisions, if it does not possess the power of learning, will be completely literal-minded. Woe to us if we let it decide our conduct, unless we have previously examined the laws of its action, and know fully that its conduct will be carried out on principles acceptable to us! On the other hand, the machine like the *djinnee* (genie), which can learn and can make decisions on the basis of its learning, will in no way be obliged to make such decisions as we should have made, or as will be acceptable to us. For the man who is not aware of this, to throw the problem of his responsibility on the machine, whether it can learn or not, is to cast his responsibility to the winds, and to find it coming back seated on the whirlwind." (W)

If the machines are purely in the control of a handful of corporations, the entire structure will be designed to their advantage.

The Job Versus the Role

Both Wiener and McLuhan saw the dawn of the era of automation and asked the question, what happens to the job?

> "Such is also the harsh logic of industrial automation. All that we had previously achieved mechanically by great exertion and coordination can now be done electrically without effort. Hence the specter of joblessness and propertylessness in the electric age. Wealth and work become information factors, and **totally new structures are needed** to run a business or relate it to social needs and markets." (Mc)

Certainly such technological transformation is not unprecedented. According to the BLS, a century and half ago, over 60% of the American populace was engaged directly in farming, today that number is 1.5%. In the 1950s, at the height of American industry, a third of the population was directly involved in manufacturing, today that number is less than 8%. In the last half-century, wealth has been violently transferred to the Tech sector, yet it employs less than 2% of the workforce. To this point, Tech has greatly been valued for the labor it displaces.

> "Thus, with automation, for example, the new patterns of human association tend to eliminate jobs, it is true. That is the negative result. Positively, automation creates roles for people, which is to say depth of involvement in their work and human association that our preceding mechanical technology had destroyed. Many people would be disposed to say that it was not the machine, but what one did with the machine, that was its meaning or message. In terms of the ways in which the machine altered our relations to one another and to ourselves, it

mattered not in the least whether it turned out cornflakes or Cadillacs." (Mc)

McLuhan's point, his refutation of Sarnoff, is essential to any understanding of the politics of technology. Technology's adoption, no matter what technology, no matter what its content, asserts political aspects in and of itself. The political structures built atop and through this technology need to take into account a technology's politics to effectively design the greater political environment. For example, America's Agrarian Era government institutions changed not at all with American industrialization. Whatever democratic character the institutions originally had were largely lost. The 19th century community associations built around agriculture, that Tocqueville understood as essential elements of democracy in America, largely disappeared by the middle of the 20th century, replaced by the forceful organization of the undemocratic industrial corporation and broadcast media.

At its foundation, automation, the process of feedback, is an information process that can, for certain people, require a "depth of involvement in their work and human association that our preceding mechanical technology had destroyed." However, the overwhelming number of jobs since created have been of no greater depth, in fact the economy overwhelmingly created "service" jobs, which in their responsibilities – food, entertainment, and care – a couple hundred years ago would have been designated servants work. One characteristic all servants share is they don't decide. The structural change in power that occurred with electric and information technologies has not been an empowering of the individual, but ever greater control by ever fewer massive corporations.

McLuhan writes,

"Work, however, does not exist in a nonliterate world. The primitive hunter or fisherman did no work, any more than does the poet, painter, or thinker of today. Where the whole man is involved there is no work. Work begins with the division of labor and the specialization of functions and tasks in sedentary, agricultural communities. In the computer age we are once more totally involved in our roles. In the electric age the 'job of work ' yields to dedication and commitment, as in the tribe." (Mc)

The thing McLuhan misses, and it's from ignoring political organization, is work has been a social construct created by the dominant power entities of each era. A switch from the job to roles, requires a complete restructuring of existing associations, corporations, and government, in order to value the role and not the job. This next generation of information technology marketed as AI will facilitate not just the automation of blue collar jobs, but even more quickly many designated white collar jobs.

"Let us remember that the automatic machine, whatever we think of any feelings it may have or may not have, is the precise economic equivalent of slave labor. Any labor which competes with slave labor must accept the economic conditions of slave labor." (W)

The role, opposed to the job, requires organization that values participation, and most especially participation in decision making.

"The village had institutionalized all human functions in forms of low intensity. In this mild form everyone could play many roles. Participation was high, and organization was low. This is the formula for stability in any type of organization." (Mc)

This is an exceptional point, the greater the participation, the lesser necessity for strict organization, either by law, the assembly line, or bureaucratic centralized order of the corporation or government. Social order, stability, societal homeostasis can be provided through active participation, not just by stringent rules. Such order is not only anathema to centralized power, but requires a great relearning and redefining of the roles of all involved.

"In the age of instant information man ends his job of fragmented specializing and assumes the role of information gathering. Today information gathering resumes the inclusive
concept of "culture," exactly as the primitive food-gatherer
worked in complete equilibrium with his entire environment.
Our quarry now, in this new nomadic and "work-less world, is
knowledge and insight into the creative processes of life and
society." (Mc)

Looking at the culture of the internet, McLuhan was absolutely
correct. People now spend hours every day "information gathering."
Yet, this is not a participation in creation, actively organizing, or decision making, but mostly that of the passive consumer and the animal
lost in the hypnotizing light of the screen. In order for information
gathering to be effectively incorporated into participatory roles
requires a reorganization, a redesign of established institutions and
processes making them controlled by participation. There is no talk of
this. For the great mass of humanity, the screen attached to infinite
information becomes nothing more than an ever more dominant
diversion.

Specialists and Generalists

The greatest change electric networked information technologies
beget is a loosening of specialist control, requiring more whole,
systemic views. As McLuhan notes this change goes deep, much
deeper, into the ubiquitous divisional order of society.

"In education the conventional division of the curriculum into
subjects is already as outdated as the medieval trivium and
quadrivium after the Renaissance. Any subject taken in depth at
once relates to other subjects. Continued in their present
patterns of fragmented unrelation, our school curricula will
insure a citizenry unable to understand the cybernated world in
which they live." (Mc)

Ignorance of the whole goes from bottom to top of our specialized society. In the Industrial Era, specialization, coined by Adam Smith as the division of labor, allowed magnitudes of success with no knowledge of the larger world than a specific specialization. It was exemplified in academia. "Even specialist learning in higher education proceeds by ignoring interrelationships; for such complex awareness slows down the achieving of expertness." (Mc) In opposition, "we need a range of thought that will really unite the different sciences, shared among a group of men who are thoroughly trained, each in his own field, but who also possess a competent knowledge of adjoining fields." (W) Only politics can provide such whole views.

"Perhaps it would not be a bad idea for the teams at present creating cybernetics to add to their cadre of technicians, who have come from all horizons of science, some serious anthropologists, and perhaps a philosopher who has some curiosity as to world matters." (W)

Again, this is not simply a need of the Tech industry or academia, but requires a reorganization of all our institutions, an acknowledgment general knowledge is part of the education and responsibility of every citizen, an understanding the specialist, the expert lacks knowledge of their specialty's connections to the rest of the world. These connections are politics.

In the last half-century with identity politics, specialization and division have come to dominate politics itself, brought about in part by electric media.

"For most people, their own ego image seems to have been typographically conditioned, so that the electric age with its return to inclusive experience threatens their idea of self. These are the fragmented ones, for whom specialist toil renders the mere prospect of leisure or jobless security a nightmare. Electric simultaneity ends specialist learning and activity, and demands interrelation in depth, even of the personality." (Mc)

The dominance of specialist organization has created just the opposite reaction. People cling to increasingly anachronistic, specialized cultural identities, while the necessity of politics in establishing a greater whole societal identity, the necessity of an encompassing human identity in regards to our relation to technology and the environment is degraded, lost, or simply never existed.

Values

The greatest task before humanity in this era of great technological change is not the development of new technology, but reformed social reorganization incorporating human values, not simply values defined by the technology or those of leviathan corporations. A reorganization recognizing a renaissance of values not simply of the last century or two, but some going back tens of thousands years, can help provide a greater understanding of ourselves.

> "In connection with the effective amount of communal information, one of the most surprising facts about the body politic is its extreme lack of efficient homeostatic processes. There is a belief, current in many countries, which has been elevated to the rank of an official article of faith in the United States, that free competition is itself a homeostatic process: that in a free market the individual selfishness of the bargainers, each seeking to sell as high and buy as low as possible, will result in the end in a stable dynamics of prices, and with redound to the greatest common good. This is associated with the very comforting view that the individual entrepreneur, in seeking to forward his own interest, is in some manner a public benefactor and has thus earned the great rewards with which society has showered him. Unfortunately, the evidence, such as it is, is against this simpleminded theory." (W Cy)

This simpleminded theory overwhelmingly provides the dominant, even exclusive, value of our era even more so than Wiener's, with the tech innovator valued only as entrepreneur. It is the organizational value of our dominant institutions.

> "It may very well be a good thing for humanity to have the machine remove from it the need of menial and disagreeable tasks, or it may not. I do not know. It cannot be good for these new potentialities to be assessed in the terms of the market, of the money they save; and it is precisely the terms of the open market, the 'fifth freedom,' that have become the shibboleth of the sector of American opinion represented by the National Association of Manufacturers and the Saturday Evening Post. I say American opinion, for as an American, I know it best, but the hucksters recognize no national boundary." (W Cy)

Today, hucksters run the show.

A first step in reorganizing our institutions, a revaluing, is understanding centralization, hierarchical organization is not simply endemic but considered natural.

> "In this, our view of society differs from the ideal of society which is held by many Fascists, Strong Men in Business, and Government. Similar men of ambition for power are not entirely unknown in scientific and educational institutions. Such people prefer an organization in which all orders come from above, and none return. The human beings under them have been reduced to the level of effectors for a supposedly higher nervous organism. ...in my mind, any use of a human being in which less is demanded of him and less is attributed to him than his full status is a degradation and a waste. It is a degradation to a human being to chain him to an oar and use him as a source of power; but it is an almost equal degradation to assign him a purely repetitive task in a factory, which demands less than a millionth of his brain capacity. It is simpler to organize a factory or galley which uses individual human beings for a trivial fraction of their worth than it is to provide a world in which they can grow to their full stature. Those who

suffer from a power complex find the mechanization of man a simple way to realize their ambitions. I say, that this easy path to power is in fact not only a rejection of everything that I consider to be of moral worth in the human race, but also a rejection of our now very tenuous opportunities for a considerable period of human survival." (W)

This prevalent centralized, undemocratic, degrading value of humanity requires politics to change. A politics that values people as people first and institutes organization allowing them to fully participate in creating the collective whole, in turn defining each person, in short democracy.

"Electric technology is directly related to our central nervous systems, so it is ridiculous to talk of 'what the public wants' played over its own nerves. This question would be like asking people what sort of sights and sounds they would prefer around them in an urban metropolis! Once we have surrendered our senses and nervous systems to the private manipulation of those who would try to benefit from taking a lease on our eyes and ears and nerves, we don't really have any rights left. Leasing our eyes and ears and nerves to commercial interests is like handing over the common speech to a private corporation, or like giving the earth's atmosphere to a company as a monopoly. Something like this has already happened with outer space, for the same reasons that we have leased our central nervous systems to various corporations. As long as we adopt the Narcissus attitude of regarding the extensions of our own bodies as really out there and really independent of us, we will meet all technological challenges with the same sort of banana-skin pirouette and collapse." (Mc)

Today, the entire media of communication and the rest of the economy is centrally controlled by a handful of corporations. A politics of technology begins with restructuring control of technology using the technology itself. We need to contemplate how we reform traditional pyramidal social structures with power concentrated at the top and control extending in one direction to a more distributed, horizontally networked organization with power distributed and control gained by continuous feedback across the network. Through this structure order is gained and just as imperatively value. Participation continually defines and redefines both order and value.

"All organizations, but especially biological ones, struggle to remain constant in their inner condition amidst the variations of outer shock and change. The man-made social environment as an extension of man's physical body is no exception. The city, as a form of the body politic, responds to new pressures and irritations by resourceful new extensions always in the effort to exert staying power, constancy, equilibrium, and homeostasis." (Mc)

"The implosion of electric energy in our century cannot be met by explosion or expansion, but it can be met by decentralism and the flexibility of multiple small centers. For example, the rush of students into our universities is not explosion but implosion. And the needful strategy to encounter this force is not to enlarge the university but to create numerous groups of autonomous colleges in place of our centralized university plant that grew up on the lines of European government and nineteenth-century industry." (Mc)

A half-century after this implosion of students into universities, the expanded university is incapable of offering anything but the most specialized education. Any sort of more generalized knowledge made valueless by established social structures whether they're cultural, political, government, or, and especially, the corporation.

"Plato, who had old-fashioned tribal ideas of political structure, said that the proper size of a city was indicated by the number of people who could hear the voice of a public speaker. Even the printed book, let alone radio, renders the political

assumptions of Plato quite irrelevant for practical purposes."
(Mc)

Or as James Madison, the principal architect of the American constitution, wrote two thousand years later, "In a democracy, the people meet and exercise the government in person; in a republic, they assemble and administer it by their representatives and agents. A democracy, consequently, will be confined to a small spot." It needs to be pointed out this organizational distinction between democracies and republics was something Madison made-up. Nonetheless, what are the political implications for political organization allowed by the internet and this next generation of networked compute technologies? It requires not simply a reform of organization but a reform of value, value defined through participation.

The Organic Planet

We require not simply an understanding of machines' interactions with the species *Homo sapiens*, but also the machines' interaction with the larger environment, the ecological systems by which human beings remain very much defined, no matter how our technology alters it. "The process of receiving and of using information is the process of our adjusting to the outer environment, and of our living effectively under that environment." (W)

From the beginning until today, human technological development has ignored and dismissed the environmental implications and impacts of technology. In fact, just the opposite, the mindset has largely been that of conquering nature, simply an impossibility as we are nature. The Industrial Era saw a massive transformation of the global environment, a transformation continuing even as the feedback from its destructive power grows in severity. We now develop new technologies in response to the impact of older technologies. "We have modified our environment so radically that we must now modify ourselves in order to exist in the new environment." (W Cy)

The latest response to this long established exclusive linear mindset is the idea humanity can flee the planet, the world which created and defines us, wrapped in our own technological shell, Narcissus in space. Simultaneously, we remain vastly ignorant of both ourselves and the greater environment that created us. The next generation of technology would best develop by not trying to conquer the world, but in appreciation of it.

THE BOOK AND THE SCREEN

In Tocqueville's *Ancien Regime* there's an excellent chapter titled, "How around the middle of the eighteenth century men of letters became the leading political figures in the country and the consequences of this." It's a wonderful explanation of the unequaled importance books and their authors played in the French Revolution. Anyone with elementary knowledge of the times can quickly begin a list of the authors including Voltaire, Rousseau, and Montesquieu, the list is long. Most enchanting, Tocqueville places the fundamental catalyst for the Revolution in the authors' pens.

Tocqueville writes,

> "All the spirit of political opposition aroused by the failings of government had taken refuge in literature since it could not thrive in public affairs. Writers had become the authentic leaders of that great gathering which leaned towards demolition of the social and political institutions of the country."

Before this chapter, Tocqueville spends two-thirds of the book explaining the long deterioration and increasing failure of French government and politics. 18th century France saw the disenfranchisement of the old feudal nobility, who were gradually stripped of responsibility but gathered ever greater privileges, the complete isolation of the peasantry, and the total centralization of government power under a rapacious crown. He explains,

> "Now when you think that this same French nation so alienated from its own affairs, so deprived of experience, so hindered by its own institutions and so helpless to reform them was, at the

same time, of all nations on earth, the most literary and the most fond of intellectual things, you will easily realize how writers became a political influence at that time and ended by being the most important."

He continues,

"All men chafing from the daily practice of legislation soon fell in love with this literary form of politics. The taste for it affected even those whose nature and social position naturally kept them as far away as possible from abstract speculations. Not a single taxpayer bruised by the uneven distribution of the *taille* (tax) was not warmed by the idea that all men should be equal; any small landowner stripped bare by an aristocratic neighbor's rabbits was pleased to hear that every kind of privilege without exception was condemned by reason. Each public enthusiasm was thus cloaked in philosophy; public life was forced into literature. Writers took hold of public opinion and found themselves for a time occupying the position which party leaders usually occupied in free countries."

The political ascendance of the writer was brought about not only by the failure of established politics, but just as importantly the rise of the influence of the book/pamphlet. Over the last several centuries, feudal institutions and customs had degraded and became politically disenfranchised. The rise of the book occurred with and helped cause this decline. The book, the product of the printing press, was a post-feudal technology.

Tocqueville describes the political decline and the resulting reaction,

"On seeing so many bizarre and disordered institutions – the offspring of other eras – which seemed bound to live forever even when they lost their value, writers readily conceived a distaste for ancient ways and tradition and were naturally drawn to a desire to rebuild the society of their time following an entirely new plan which each of them traced by the light of his reason alone."

The *Ancien Regime* records the impotence of French politics as an entirely inert force. "A French nation so alienated from its own affairs, so deprived of experience, so hindered by its own institutions and so helpless to reform." A situation not far in the distance for American politics. Into this void the writer stepped, not so much by acclaim, as necessity.

Across the globe, the book helped play a defining political role for the next two centuries. Yet in 21st century America, books and writers are politically inconsequential. In the last fifty years, you'd be hard pressed to name a book or writer that has consequentially impacted politics, in the last two decades, not one.

This is neither a fault of the books or writers. I can immediately name a couple excellent books just in the last half dozen years, Yasha Levine's *Surveillance Valley* and Alexander Zaitchik's *Owning the Sun* that should be widely influential in the creation of any consequential political thinking for the 21st century. Both disappeared almost as quickly as they were published. The reason the book no longer influences politics is twofold; first, just as with 18th century France, the decline of anything that can be considered healthy politics, secondly, the screen's conquest of the book.

The screen is a new invention, not much more than a century old compared to the seven century history of the printing press. The screen was introduced with the invention of film. It was projected upon, a collective experience of hundreds seated in theaters. Fifty years later, with television, the screen inverted. The screen itself and the collective viewing experience shrunk in size moving from theaters to homes. However, thanks to broadcast technology, audiences could simultaneously be tens of millions of people scattered across family rooms in millions of homes. In the last two decades, screens have shrunk to fit into a pocket, the experience shrinking to one person connected to a continuous and might as well be considered an infinite data stream capable of being tapped at the individual's discretion.

While the screen can be a text medium, as anyone reading this can attest, it is a much more powerful medium of images and attached sound. The screen has not simply displaced the book's political role but trampled it. Interestingly, despite the screen's illusion of total immersion in the world, it has created an Ancien Regime politics where individuals have "no connection with that world nor *can* they see what others *are* doing in it" and "*lack* the obvious education which the sight of a free society and the news of what is happening give even to those with the least contact with government."

Despoiling the politics preceding it, the screen created personalities. Personality isn't politics, but personalities can be marketed. A half-century ago, the great technology historian Marshall McLuhan made an astute observation on the screen's development and society, "Full awareness of this technological change had dawned on Madison Avenue ten years ago when it shifted its tactics from the promotion of the individual product to the collective involvement in the 'corporate image.'"

This has become the social aspect of the screen, individual personality/image as corporatized product, defined collectively through the use of the tools of business, mainly marketing and advertising. Tocqueville wrote, "Writers took hold of public opinion and found themselves for a time occupying the position which party leaders usually occupied in free countries." Today, the screen is the only party, comprised of partisanly marketed personalities/images. Organization, the fundamental element of all effective politics, is simply the screen, the organization behind the personalities politically ignored.

The 18th century book, their writers, and their ideas helped overthrow the Ancien Regime, but failed entirely in creating a new French political order. The same books, writers, and ideas simultaneously helped shape the new American republic. There's many reasons for this, deserving a book themselves, but one very important reason just as important for this age, the American revolutionaries were never "contemptuous of ancient wisdom and still more inclined to trust their own reason." The American revolutionaries were steeped in historical knowledge. The democratic histories of Ancient Athens and Rome was wisdom they sought to enshrine in building a new age of politics. At its founding, the American republic, unlike the French, did not claim to abolish the past and proclaim a new Year 1. Today's Silicon Valley tech revolutionaries have more in common with 1789 Paris than 1776 Philadelphia.

The Ancien Regime of France was overthrown by the book and the book shaped the modern world. McLuhan writes,

> "....typographic technology, applied not only to the rationalizing of the entire procedures of production and marketing, but to law and education and city planning, as well. The principles of continuity, uniformity, and repeatability derived from print technology have, in England and America, long permeated every phase of communal life."

He adds, "Literacy is indispensable for habits of uniformity at all times and places. Above all, it is needed for the workability of price systems and markets." The screen is now in the process of overthrowing all this, text has not disappeared, but fitfully survives on the screen, increasingly only as a select medium of power. As McLuhan writes, "the screen child encounters the world in a spirit antithetic to literacy." It is immensely ironic that for two centuries, the republican revolutions across the globe called in unison for universal literacy, while the first modern republic, America, experiences the dominance of the screen and the displacement of literacy as any sort of political medium.

To in any way confront this reality requires first and foremost an understanding it is happening. In 21st century America, the screen has destroyed established politics as thoroughly as the book helped overthrow France's 18th century Ancien Regime. The impulses of those controlling the organization behind the screen are not in any way republican, but Napoleonic. Understanding the screen and figuring out how to incorporate it into a healthy politics is fundamental for any notions of democracy in the 21st century.

MISTAH KURTZ – HE DEAD.

"The great wall of vegetation, an exuberant and entangled mass of trunks, branches, leaves, boughs, festoons, motionless in the moonlight, was like a rioting invasion of soundless life, a rolling wave of plants, piled up, crested, ready to topple over the creek, to sweep every little man of us out of his little existence."

— JOSEPH CONRAD, *HEART OF DARKNESS*

Say whatever else you will about *Homo sapiens*, we are not good at complexity. Our conceptions of life, particularly much of what's considered knowledge, are adept at generalization. Single components are often used in attempt to simply define complex systems which they are only a part. We grasp a part, one specific aspect of an intricately, immeasurably entangled system, such as an ecological system or even one particular in the internal workings of a single biological organism, then claim understanding. It cannot be denied in such division there is certain, even great power to then shape and form, move and build. Yet single pieces of knowledge never provide a whole understanding of whatever complex system they were derived.

Every technology simplifies complexity. Every technology is a literal hammer pounding a specific nail. Again, this in no way denies the power of any given technology, in many ways just the opposite, technology is a testimony to the abilities of the human intellect to form and wield the power of simple homogenized force. The revolutionary experience of the Industrial Era was the use of uniform force to reshape complex environments around any given single technology, resulting in a simpler, less complex order.

Joseph Conrad's sublime novel *Heart of Darkness* can be read as an allegory of humanity's struggle with complexity, most especially the seeming chaos of nature meeting industrial uniformity. Conrad beautifully describes nature's complexity as the jungle "rioting." Rioting is an excellently astute term for humanity's general perception of complexity using both Webster's definitions of "a random or disorderly profusion" and "a violent public disorder."

With this idea of rioting, Conrad expresses the deep human fear of nature, particularly since the dawn of the Agrarian Era when nature became separate, that is the world beyond human society, constantly threatening our imposed order. It is nature as undomesticated savagery, disorder we seek to order. Order in *Heart of Darkness* is civilization represented by the Company and its homogenization of all value based on one measure — the pursuit of profit from ivory. This is the novel's greatest and darkest destructive force.

Heart of Darkness is based on the brutal imperial rule of the Belgians over the Congo. In the long, horrendously bloody annals of European imperialism, the Belgian Congo was a particularly horrid affair. Marlow, the book's protagonist, hooks up with the Company headquartered in a Belgian city described as a "white sepulcher," for a trip up the Congo river, not as an imperialist, but an adventurer. Meeting the Company's semi-mythical best employee, Kurtz, becomes his quest.

The Company's hopeless, singular nihilistic drive representing European imperialism is first observed manifested in the trip down the African coast to the Congo's mouth. Marlow encounters various European outposts hanging onto the African coast in varying degrees of disarray, depravity, and decay. At times, the ship engages Europe's greatest technology to worthlessly fire its guns into the jungle. Marlow remarks "in the empty immensity of earth, sky, and water, there she was, incomprehensible, firing into a continent." He observes the whole affair has "a touch of insanity in the proceeding, a sense of lugubrious drollery in the sight."

As he heads up the river, Marlow asks of the jungle, "Could we handle that dumb thing, or would it handle us? I felt how big, how confoundedly big, was that thing that couldn't talk, and perhaps was deaf as well. What was in there?" The incomprehensibility of the jungle's complexity holds no darkness, paradoxically it lies in the very understandably simple, single value of the Company. Marlow illuminates on the Company, "In the blinding sunshine of that land I would become acquainted with a flabby, pretending, weak-eyed devil of a rapacious and pitiless folly." He adds, "To tear treasure out of the bowels of the land was their desire, with no more moral purpose at the back of it than there is in burglars breaking into a safe."

As for the people of the Congo, in the words of the Company's accountant, "When one has got to make correct entries, one comes to hate those savages — hate them to the death." Measured with such a uniform, singular value, Kurtz's unmatched ability to collect ivory makes him a "prodigy," in the European imperial sense "an emissary of pity and science and progress," who Marlow discovers has not in the old colonial expression gone native, but savage. Kurtz's bloody obsession with being the most productive ivory collector becomes the rationale for a brutal and savage rule — "The work was going on. The work!"

The power and limits of 19th century European technology within the vast complexity of nature is one of the book's tragedies, though Conrad is not simply talking about technology but the great nihilism of Western imperialism. The true immorality lie not up the Congo, but the Thames, to London, where lies "the heart of an immense darkness."

"All Europe contributed to the making of Kurtz," the homogenizing force of European civilization is represented by technology and the singularity of value measured in profit with the collection of ivory. The inability to value beyond this singular, uniform measure, allows both the Company and Kurtz to descend into savagery. Maybe, this greatest sin is best expressed in "Apocalypse Now," Francis Ford Coppola's surreal film adaptation of Conrad's book. In the film, it is not the Belgians and Brits in the Congo, but Americans who rain down the brute, brutal, uniform force of modern technological savagery onto the jungles and peoples of South East Asia. Captain Willard (Marlow), now of the American army, Kurtz's commissioned executioner rationalizes, "Even the jungle wanted him dead."

Marlow opines on Kurtz's deviance, "Those heads on a stake would have been even more impressive if their faces had not been turned toward the house." Kurtz's "unsound method," his "no method at all" is completely anathema to the jungle's complexity, where method, innumerable methods comprise every action.

Heart of Darkness is filled with the images and consequences of the force of Western uniformity, the powerfully destructive homogeneity of industrial technology in opposition to what Conrad describes as the "inscrutable intention" of nature's complexity. Yet in the last century, the opacity of nature's complexity has begun to be revealed.

In *The Secret Network of Nature,* Peter Wohlleben writes,

"When we see just how multilayered the interactions between different species are, we have to ask, once again, whether we will ever be able to fully comprehend the connections in our environment. The examples we've discussed so far involve just a few animals influencing each other in highly complex ways. Every time a new species enters the act, things become much more complicated and difficult to follow."

A century later, Wohlleben's understanding of nature's complexity is certainly greater than Conrad's "invasion of soundless life." Though still superficial, our growing knowledge of nature's complexity in many ways has revealed a completely contradictory understanding to many of our established and revered ideas of order. Our interactions with nature, especially in regards to technology, remain simplistic and require greater understanding of nature's complexity in our culture, politics, and economics.

Wohlleben writes,

"What is nature? One simple standard definition is that nature is the opposite of culture—that is to say, everything that people have not created or changed. This definition draws hard and fast boundaries around what can be called nature. Other defini- tions see people and their activities as part of nature. From this perspective, nature and culture cannot be clearly separated."

This latter understanding of nature is a beginning. Humanity and every action we initiate are part of nature. We do nothing unnatural. Our technologies might be unprecedented, but never unnatural. If these technologies destroy long established systems, this is not unnat- ural, even though it leads to further extinction of species and the destruction of complex ancient ecological systems. Eventually, it may very well lead to the destruction of the human culture that created the technology, threatening the survival of the species *Homo sapiens* itself, but then we've only been around a few hundred thousand years on a planet that's been orbiting this radiant star for over 4.5 billion years.

Technologies developed from our less than a century knowledge of quantum physics and biology directly insert nature's complexity into the technologies and thus into human society as a whole, complexities that few, if any, truly understand. We quickly pile these new technologies atop two centuries old industrial infrastructures, infrastructures that transformed human life and reshaped numerous ecological systems in ways we still little understand or refuse to grasp. Today, nature's "inscrutable intention" internally reshapes human society.

Can we devise complex social systems, better reflecting both the complexity of nature and our rapidly developing contemporary technologies? Most specifically, can we evolve governance? This is a question mostly ignored for the past century, outside brief flirtations with a sort of neo-Incan, industrial communism. With modernity, the great revolution of governance was the reintroduction of ancient republicanism, which proves increasingly insufficient and failing in regards to healthily influencing technological development, among plenty of other things.

The problem goes back well beyond republicanism to the birth and development of government itself. From the beginning, governance not simply shunned complexity, but actively sought to diminish it. The history of recorded government goes hand in hand with the rise of agrarianism, humanity's first powerful technological homogenizing of nature's complexity, promoting an ever decreasing selection of plants and animals.

Central control can only be realized via uniform, commanded standards, whether beliefs, laws, processes, or technologies. The need for standardization helped develop seemingly eternal cultural laws and commandments upheld by the rule of heavenly bestowed kings and emperors. Unlike the constantly interacting, ever evolving chaos, the rioting of nature, centralized governance sought to represent the immovable, the permanent.

Only for limited and relatively brief times in recorded history, with systems of democracy, did government become less stringent and more flexible, accomplished with government structures and processes demanding greater citizen participation, thus greater complexity, somewhat paradoxically accomplished atop a general ethos of citizen equality. However, modern republicanism sought to wrap itself in government's traditional mantle of permanence. The great democratic thinker Hannah Arendt noted many of the American founders sought to create a system of government for the ages. Modern republicanism could not gain legitimacy through ancient government notions of a supposed unchanging past, but through an eternal, unchanging future. The constitution became enshrined.

Thomas Jefferson, alone among America's founding pantheon, thought each generation should amend and restructure government. "Earth belongs to the living" and governance must evolve so "laws and institutions go hand in hand with progress of the human mind." Creating a more complex democratic structure "is not to trust it all to one; but to divide it among the many, distributing to every one exactly the functions he is competent to." Jefferson understood democracy is directly opposite "the generalisng and concentrating all cares and powers into one body, no matter whether of the Autocrats of Russia or France, or of the Aristocrats of a Venetian Senate," and today's militaristic, corporate oligarchy of Washington DC.

In two letters, both written in 1816, he briefly outlined ideas for expanding democracy with the idea of "ward republics" instituted "by dividing and subdividing these republics from the great National one down thro' all its subordinations."

Jefferson continues,

"The elementary republics of the wards, the county republics, the State republics, and the republic of the Union, would form a gradation of authorities, standing each on the basis of law, holding every one its delegated share of powers, and constituting truly a system of fundamental balances and checks for the government."

This essential understanding concerning checks and balances necessary for any self-government is lost to American education. It wasn't just the three branches of government in Washington that served as checks and balances against concentration of unwarranted power, but just as importantly the structures of state and local government. Just as check and balances now fail in every respect in Washington, the checks and balances of local and state government were previously lost over the last century and half with the processes of industrialization and power ever more greatly concentrated in DC.

Jefferson's thought is constrained by the notion of gradient power, the ancient idea of centralized, hierarchical, pyramid shaped government order. Yet, it was also Jefferson amongst the enshrined founders who warned the constitution insured the gradual centralization of all political power in the Federal government. Forty years later, he concluded constitutional reform required the "division and subdivision of duties alone, that all matters, great & small, can be managed to perfection and the whole is cemented by giving to every citizen personally a part in the administration of the public affairs" – democratic complexity.

Though of the Enlightenment, Jefferson lived before the great industrial technological revolution. He was completely bereft of any understanding of the underlying importance of the political shaping forces of technology. He writes,

"Let it be agreed that a government is republican in proportion as every member composing it has his equal voice in the direction of its concerns, (not indeed in person, which would be impracticable beyond the limits of a city, or small township)."

The century after Jefferson's death saw industrial and then broadcast technologies completely transcend, redefine, and make meaningless the established limits of township, city, state, and nation.

In the past century, knowledge gained through physics and biology completely upended ancient notions of any centralized control in nature. The organization of fundamental physical particles and energy, of organisms and ecologies worked completely opposite. Order rises not from the top but from below, through the constant interaction of distributedly networked atoms and cells. It's nature's reality of distributedly networked order, complexity, which can allow government to evolve and provide democratic capabilities to influence the development of technologies based on this very same knowledge of natural order. If only influenced by centralized, uniform political order, including the power of mega-corporations, technology will increasingly become distorted, harmful, and dangerous. Also, it is basically assured centralized control will become incapable of either advantageously directing technological complexity or systemically reacting robustly to its implementation.

The great political questions of our times are how humanity reorganizes institutions, both government and private, to be distributedly networked, that is to better mimic nature's order. It requires a reforming of physical organization and just as imperatively evolving how we socially process information. The US has an advantage in that it still has a robust local government infrastructure. A gradual devolution can take place, moving political power from DC and state governments back to the local level. Simultaneously, local governments must begin to be horizontally networked together, learning to act together in concert on many matters, while independently being allowed to take advantage of local environments.

Local government itself needs to be restructured to become much more participatory. Social, political, economic and cultural structures would become more participatory and distributedly networked. Humanity needs to create a global distributed information system, maybe metaphorically thought of as a global nervous system or complex ecological system. With limited understanding how to accomplish this, it will be an organic process evolving around need and success.

All nodes of this vast, complex, largely horizontal network would create and edit information, constantly communicating both internally and across the network, incessantly making decisions. It requires democratic methods of controlling information, a necessity of open access and free movement. Technological and information standards need to be open. Copyrights and patents need to be reassessed. In short, a revaluation of the value of information based not exclusively or even primarily on entrenched, uniform, industrial economic thinking or centralized government's ancient notion of controlling information, but information access and implementation in relation to the beneficial development of human needs, democracy, and technology.

The greatest change such a networked society offers in regards to technological development is a cyclical system where feedback is valued to as great a degree as initiation, unlike industrialization's ignoring feedback of the complex ecological systems we altered. It is a reformation of society, technological and process development better fit to nature's complexity. Doing so requires evolving the idea of government's foundation on eternal commandments, unalterable decrees, and fixed laws to one much more malleable, consistently evolving through ceaseless interaction. Permanence comes in assembly, the nodes of the network, that is the people themselves, as Jefferson stated "the whole is cemented by giving to every citizen personally a part in the administration of the public affairs."

No doubt jettisoning ideas of unalterable permeance and central-ized authority cause great consternation, agitated chattering, and a sickness unto death, as the scrawny, nervous Dane decried. But fear and tremble not, there's no need to completely discard or dismiss the idea of uniformity or of unwavering principles, but they need to be derived out of the understanding of the basic, shared, equal funda-mental nature of each of us as part of the species *Homo sapiens* and our relation with nature's complexity.

In many ways the symbolic father of this new era, J. Robert Oppen-heimer claimed with all the change of the last several centuries since the advancement of knowledge under the Scientific Revolution "there remains no gospel greater than Saint Mathew's or the Bhagavad Gita." So, after two-thousand years, why not try implementing the golden rule, "Do unto others as you would have them do unto you," as a foun-dational societal ethos. That alone would initiate a political revolution, confronting and overcoming of the savage in each and every one of us.

Homo sapiens evolved from and remain defined by the complexities of nature. For millennia, our technologies have grown into increasingly powerful forces shaping us individually and socially, simultaneously restructuring, much of it destructively, the natural world that birthed us. The last half-century witnesses nature's complexity growing in the technologies themselves, requiring a political embrace of complexity.

Mistah Kurtz – he dead.

UNNATURAL SELECTION: TECHNOLOGICAL EVOLUTION

"The ordinary person senses the greatness of the odds against him even without thought or analysis, and he adapts his attitudes unconsciously. A huge passivity has settled on industrial society. For people carried about in mechanical vehicles, earning their living by waiting on machines, listening much of the waking day to canned music, watching packaged movie entertainment and capsulated news, for such people it would require an exceptional degree of awareness and an especial heroism of effort to be anything but supine consumers of processed goods."

— MARSHALL MCLUHAN, *THE MECHANICAL BRIDE: FOLKLORE OF INDUSTRIAL MAN*

The 21st century is a revolutionary era for humanity and technology, but not in the way most think. We watch, and most are simply watching, technology increasingly developed in reaction to environments created by previous technology. Going back millions of years in the history of hominids, from the capture of fire and flaking of stone tools, technological innovation was about altering the environment of the planet which birthed us. Recently, by historical measures, after two centuries of industrial development, humanity develops more and more technology in response to environments created by older technology.

The FT has a good piece on using genetic engineering in response to climate and ecological changes effected by industrial technologies. A Dutch farmer succinctly sums up, "Climate change is coming faster than we are developing new crops. We need new techniques. There is a big danger to food production in Europe."

The FT explains further,

"Widespread drought has cut harvests across Europe, with Spain losing half its olive crop. The war in Ukraine has reduced exports from a country dubbed the bread basket of Europe. The drought and conflict, combined with high energy costs, have driven up food prices and caused shortages in the developing world."

Initiated ten-thousand years ago, the Agrarian Revolution was humanity's greatest technological innovation, altering much of the planet's environment, and in the process creating new societal organization – tilled lands instituted cities. With the introduction of industrial technologies and techniques, agriculture was radically transformed.

The technologies and techniques of industrial agriculture are shaped and powered by fossil fuels. They can be divided into three main categories: 1) mechanization of sowing and reaping; 2) mass application of petrochemical herbicides and pesticides; 3) manufactured fertilizers, particularly from ammonia — an energy intensive process combining atmospheric nitrogen and hydrogen from natural gas. These processes transformed farming, radically altering the greater ecological systems, much of them detrimentally. Most of these impacts are just beginning to be accounted.

The FT's Dutch potato farmer's crop is dependent on both irrigation — supply limited due to recent drought — and the rising price of fossil fuels — supply impacted by an egregiously stupid and needless war. The farmer's "outlays were up 25 per cent, he says, because of the high price of gas. Fuel for tractors, fertilisers and pesticides all got more expensive."

The article's main thrust is the agricultural industry, dominated by a handful of massive corporations, wants to meet problems manufactured by industrial technology with new biological technologies. Specifically, the article examines the technology of gene editing, "A form of genetic engineering where genes can be deleted or added from the same or similar species. It is distinct from genetic modification, which introduces DNA from foreign species."

The FT continues,

"There has been greater progress in gene editing to improve yields. Inari, a US agritech company set up in 2016, has been working on gene editing to increase yields on wheat, corn and soyabeans as well as reducing the necessary water and nitrogen fertiliser."

So, new technology derived from genetic engineering seeks to meet problems caused by technologies introduced with industrialization. Completely unrecognized is this is a major difference from the past where technologies were introduced to alter the greater environment from which *Homo sapiens* evolved. Today, we create new technologies in reaction to the environments created by older technologies.

In *Understanding Media,* the great historian of technology Marshall McLuhan stated, "Environments are not passive wrappings but active processes." This is not an industrial understanding of technology but a biological one, a Darwinian understanding. It is the recognition no technology stands alone. All technology impacts and becomes part of their greater environments – social, political, ecological, and now technological. The introduction of new technologies influences these greater environments, creating new environments that in various ways reciprocally impact the technologies themselves.

The process is perpetual. Call it unnatural selection, technological change in one place instigates change in another. The idea of perpetual change is not new to human understanding. It's an ancient one, take Heraclitus and his river for example. Yet it was lost for thousands of years then reintroduced by Darwin, but still has little impact on how we develop technology or on greater societal thinking.

For most recorded civilization, particularly concerning politics, the idea of permanence was fostered, a belief in eternal kings, laws engraved in stones, and empires upon which the sun never set. The idea of life as a constantly changing complex interrelationship, where any particular organism is only truly defined in regards to its greater environment, remains absent from both our politics and any ethos of technological development.

The FT article unknowingly or does not acknowledge the greatest of problems it documents: the complete inability of our established political structures and processes to beneficially address the questions of technological development. The FT reports massive powerful corporations advocating technologies, powerless NGOs offering limited alternatives, all to be decided by national and supranational government institutions largely controlled by the corporations.

Today, the unaccounted impact of two-centuries of industrialization demands increasing attention. In the last half-century, new knowledge fosters our ability to manipulate the very foundations of life. Unnatural selection instantaneously meets the immutable forces of Natural Selection.

In an early 1970s interview, McLuhan stated,

"When Sputnik went around the planet, nature disappeared. Nature was hijacked right off this planet. Nature was enclosed in a man made environment and art took the place of nature."

This always struck me as a most frightening perspective, one I didn't particularly care to adopt. It was extremely limited, though it can't be denied it was acutely astute. Such a perspective demanded a much better breed of artist than the technologists of the last couple generations. Along with a significantly more sophisticated, not just technologically clever civilization with a much greater respect for the nature it seeks to replace.

BINDING PROMETHEUS

"Nearly every age and stage of culture has at some time or other sought with profound irritation to free itself from the Greeks, because in their presence everything one has achieved oneself, though apparently quite original and sincerely admired, suddenly seemed to lose life and color and shriveled into a poor copy, even a caricature. And so time after time cordial anger erupts against this presumptuous little people that made bold for all time to designate everything not native as "barbaric.'"

— F. NIETZSCHE, THE BIRTH OF TRAGEDY (1872)

In the last half-century, American culture, if on cue, turned against the Greeks, a revolt succeeding in unmooring culture, casting it adrift, indeterminate in direction. The great irony, and all revolutions have their irony, the Greeks were largely responsible for the logic underlying scientific thought and its technological progeny. With the untethering from Classical Culture certain wisdom was lost. Most importantly, the lesson all knowledge gained and implemented is accompanied by certain troublesome consequences, call it tragedy.

In the poet Aeschylus' play, *Prometheus Bound*, this understanding lies at the heart of the hero's torment and trials. Prometheus is a Titan. In Greek lore, the Titans ruled the universe before the gods of Olympus – Zeus, Athena, Apollo etc. – overthrew them. Against Zeus' wishes, a dethroned Prometheus looked sympathetically on emerging humanity, bestowing upon us knowledge, science, and technology.

Prometheus gifts are best represented by fire, but he lists others,

"Yes, and numbers, too, king of sciences, I invented for them, and the combining of letters, creative mother of the Muses' arts, with which to hold all things in memory... to the chariot I harnessed horses and made them obedient to the rein, to be an image of wealth and luxury. "

Prometheus' actions outraged Zeus, who bound Prometheus upon

a high ledge and caused an eagle to continually consume his perpetu-
ally regenerating liver. Aeschylus' play was performed for the whole
city of Athens during the great annual festival to the god Dionysus,
whose worship produced Greek tragedy.

In *The Birth of Tragedy*, Friedrich Nietzsche says Prometheus' story
is a sibling to "the fall" in Genesis, where Adam and Eve upon eating
the forbidden fruit from the tree of knowledge are cast from Eden, the
cunning serpent is condemned to crawl on its belly and east dust. Nietzsche sums it up,

> "The presupposition of the Prometheus myth is primitive man's
> belief in the supreme value of fire as the true palladium of every
> rising civilization. But for man to dispose of fire freely, and not
> receive it as a gift from heaven in the kindling thunderbolt and
> the warming sunlight, seemed a crime to thoughtful primitive
> man, a despoiling of divine nature. Thus this original philosoph-
> ical problem poses at once an insoluble conflict between men
> and the gods, which lies like a huge boulder at the gateway to
> every culture. Man's highest good must be bought with a crime
> and paid for by the flood of grief and suffering which the
> offended divinities visit upon the human race in its noble
> ambition."

Knowledge lies at the foundation of tragedy. In early Greek
culture, exemplified by Aeschylus, this tragedy is celebrated. Nietzsche points out tragedy is best expressed in the dichotomy of the
two Greek gods, Apollo, representing the self-aware controlled individual, and Dionysus, who represents the chaos of the greater natural
world.

He explains of Apollo,

> "As a moral deity Apollo demands self-control from his people
> and, in order to observe such self-control, a knowledge of self.
> And so we find that the aesthetic necessity of beauty is accom-
> panied by the imperatives, 'Know thyself,' and 'Nothing too
> much.' "

In opposition is the god Dionysus, representing not the sculpted Apollonian individual, but the uncontrollable, indeterminate, endlessly changing, collective whole of nature. The Greeks understood despite our ordering knowledge, we always remained part of disordered nature. Nietzsche writes,

> "In Dionysian art and its tragic symbolism the same nature cries to us with its true, disassembled voice: 'Be as I am! Amid the ceaseless flux of phenomena I am the eternally creative primordial mother, eternally impelling to existence, eternally finding satisfaction in this change of phenomena!'"

The festival of Dionysus celebrated the loss of Apollonian individual identity in a celebratory orgy of the whole, a reminder civilization remained subservient to the greater forces of nature. Nietzsche beautifully describes the eternal interplay of the individual and this greater absolute,

> "The Dionysian and Apollonian elements, in a continuous chain of creations, each enhancing the other, dominated the Hellenic mind; how from the Iron Age, with its battles of Titans and its austere popular philosophy, there developed under the aegis of Apollo the Homeric world of beauty; how this "naïve" splendor was then absorbed once more by the Dionysian torrent, and how, face to face with this new power, the Apollonian code rigidified into the majesty of Doric art and contemplation."

Nietzsche lamented this high point of Greek culture, the embracing of tragedy, lasted only briefly, destroyed by, in what I always found most amusing, Socrates and his logical methods. Birthed from Apollo, this logic developed an idea of control not simply of the self, but of the greater natural world, eventually leading to modern humanity's misbelief we can transcend nature. Nietzsche writes of our times,

> "Our whole modern world... proposes as its ideal the theoretical man equipped with the greatest forces of knowledge, and

laboring in the service of science, whose archetype and progenitor is Socrates."

Modernity's great crime is the loss of tragedy, he criticizes, "Now we must not hide from ourselves what is concealed in the womb of this Socratic culture: optimism, with its delusion of limitless power." What better describes the culture of technology in the 21st century? Nietzsche was always the 19th century's greatest critic of the 20th century and now the 21st.

This Socratic faith was wrought by a lost appreciation of nature by the compartmentalization, not simply of the human-self, but the categorization of the whole of nature. With science and technology, the Dionysian appreciation of nature's fluidity was subsumed in the misconceived belief *Homo sapiens* can control all that surrounds us. We removed ourselves from nature by dividing and shaping. We now worship technology.

This technological separation from nature and misconstrued dominance, created massive problems in regards to the destruction of nature's womb and her teat which still nourishes. Today, the Socratic ethos of conquering and vanquishing nature seductively promises, as the snake once beguiled Eve, perpetrated technological offenses can be absolved with more technology, a mystical belief as fantastical as any ancient precedent.

Aeschylus provides a thought on how we might loosen the binds of Socratic culture. Prometheus laments his torment saying,

"Only when I have been bent by pangs and tortures infinite am I to escape my bondage. Skill is weaker by far than Necessity."

Industrialism destroyed all understanding of the underlying power of necessity, praising and rewarding the skill of the technologist, ignoring the necessity of their creations. Necessity, not skill, moves nature. In an era where energy becomes more dear, water less bountiful, and food supplies grow erratic, the inimitable power of necessity resurfaces.

Aeschylus writes,

CHORUS

"Who then is the helmsman of Necessity?"
PROMETHEUS
"The three-shaped Fates and mindful Furies."

Here the pre-Socratic Dionysian universe asserts itself. No matter our skill, we can never be separated from the forces of nature – the fates and furies – and resulting necessities. A century and half ago, the power of necessity was reintroduced to burgeoning modernity with the concept of Natural Selection. Into modernity, Dionysus reemerged, though has yet to in any way reshape our industrial Apollonian identities. Once more, the world was made complex beyond human design. Life's history is of perpetual fluidity and ceaseless motion, all change effected by another in return.

As that great Neo-Dionysian, Charles Darwin concluded, "There is grandeur in this view of life," but to experience and benefit, as both Nietzsche and the Greeks understood, its underlying tragedy must be embraced. The understanding humanity will never separate ourselves from nature requires a rebirth of tragedy. A transcending of industrial culture is possible with a focus on necessity, a renaissance of ancient wisdom.

ORACLES OF DELPHI AND CHICAGO

Delphi was the most sacred city of Ancient Greece. The Greeks considered Delphi the center of the earth. It is spectacularly situated half-way up a mountain, looking down a narrow valley widening into the Gulf of Corinth. Directly behind, rising a thousand feet, tower steep granite cliffs colored red, gray, and gold. Delphi was the sanctuary of Apollo, the sun god of music, harmony, and light. In Apollo's temple resided the Pythian oracle visited from across Greece and lands afar by supplicants looking for guidance and prophecy of the future.

Held in equal importance across the whole of Greek civilization, Apollo was the "national" god of Greece, Delphi his most hallowed temple. Every four years Delphi held a Greece-wide musical contest and athletic games known as the Pythian Games, second only to the Olympics in stature. Over the years, Delphi developed an almost

Disney-like environment. City treasuries, monuments, and statues rose from across Greece, and in later centuries from Rome, all dedicated to Apollo in gratitude for victories in battle and athletic contests, along with a variety of political and personal successes.

The Delphi founding myth stated his temple stood where the child Apollo slay Python, the great serpent protector of Gaia, the goddess of earth and mother of all life. Pythia (python) became the title of the priestess oracle. Believed to directly emanate from Apollo, the meaning of the oracle's ambiguous prognostications were very much dependent on the interpretation of the inquiring petitioner.

In many ways, the oracle might best be considered an ancient Oprah, espousing guidance for city, king, warrior, or person. The differences between the ancient Pythia and the modern Oprah say more about the two ages than the respective oracles.

The Delphic oracle appeared sometime in the 8th century BC and operated until the 4th century AD. For a thousand years, pretty much everyone who was anyone made their way to Delphi. Greek and Roman literature claim hundreds of prophecies credited to the Pythian Oracle, no doubt many apocryphal. Lycurgus, Sparta's great law giver and Athens' Solon both credited inspiration for their cities' constitutions from Delphi. In the 6th century BC, the Lydian King Croesus' prophecy rates the most infamously ambiguous. Asked if he should make war on the Persians, the oracle foretold, "A great empire would be destroyed." Unfortunately for poor Croesus, it was his empire destroyed, not the Persian's.

One of the greatest and most amusing Delphic oracles is provided by Plutarch. Four centuries after the fact, Plutarch writes in his *Lives* about the Macedonian Alexander's visit to Apollo's temple on his way to conquer the world. Plutarch writes,

"Then he went to Delphi, to consult Apollo concerning the success of the war he had undertaken, and happening to come on one of the forbidden days, when it was esteemed improper to give any answer from the oracle, he sent messengers to desire the priestess to do her office; and when she refused, on the plea of a law to the contrary, he went up himself, and began to draw her by force into the temple, until tired and overcome with his importunity, 'My son,' said she, 'thou art invincible.' Alexander taking hold of what she spoke, declared he had received such an answer as he wished for, and that it was needless to consult the god any further."

Such is the personality needed for world conquering!

A Greek, Plutarch was for a time a priest at Delphi, however this was at the end of the first-century AD. At this point, the Romans had been in control of Delphi for over two-centuries. It had seen better days. The former Treasury of Athens was now a pawnshop. Once the Romans took over in the second-century BC, Delphi began to lose its political significance with power moved to Rome. For the Greeks, the oracle's significance had been overwhelmingly political, for Rome it was largely a tourist destination, entertainment, which brings us to Oprah.

Like the Pythia, Oprah is a woman held in god-like esteem. People look to her for guidance and prophecy. However, the differences between the two, best contrast the eras. Delphi is situated in a sensationally beautiful natural setting. The Temple of Pythian Apollo, other buildings, and monuments of great variety combined to make Delphi one of the most spectacular physical sites of the ancient world.

Oprah's temple couldn't have been more different. Harpo Studios opened in a decrepit and largely abandoned warehouse district just west of Chicago's downtown. Certainly, nothing could be more dramatically in opposition than a 5th century BC walk up Delphi's Sacred Way to engage the Pythia in Apollo's Temple, than a 1990's walk down Chicago's Washington Street to "The Oprah Winfrey Show" in Harpo Studios.

This perfectly illustrates the greatest difference of the eras, the aesthetic of beautifully designed, touchable physical space replaced by the seeming ethereal magic of electric technology. Oprah had no need for an elaborately designed city or building, only a large room, with a hundred seats, lights, a small decorated stage, cameras, and a satellite dish to broadcast daily into the homes of tens of millions of Americans.

No need for pilgrimage to Chicago and Harpo Studios, just turn on the television and there, in your living room, appears the Oracle of Chicago. Unlike the Pythia, Oprah was decidedly apolitical. As a medium, television had developed decidedly unpolitical. At first controlled by three and then a handful of massive corporations, television was overwhelmingly an entertainment medium, its primary purpose to sell consumer goods produced by leviathan corporations. Oprah's supplicants needn't bring offerings to Chicago, they only needed to purchase goods from her advertisers. Oprah claimed greater wealth than all Delphi could ever dream.

Oprah preached the era's narcissistic individualism. The modern ethos of individuality devoid of greater social context, context the Greeks well understood was provided by a healthy politics – an ancient understanding of the inherent and valuable communal identity of *Homo sapiens*. As Aristotle put it, "Humankind is by nature a political animal."

Instead, and she certainly was by no means alone but vastly influential, Oprah guided her largely female adherents to fill their experiential social void, created by modernity's destruction of formerly established community, by looking within themselves, not outward with active participation in recreating a greater society. She populated her shows with self-help gurus, whacked psychology, new age mysticism, and celebrity worship – modernity's gods.

Oprah touched little on politics, though many sought her blessing, or tangentially, such as when Tipper Gore talked about her fight with depression. Hey Tipper! Here's a clue. You're married to Al. Oprah's few direct political engagements proved at very best problematic. Then in 2004, Oprah best defined the modern oracle by giving every member of her audience a car. What better prescription to make an American whole? It is not a coincidence our popular Tech oracles are still automobile prophets.

The greatest difference between ancient oracles and today's are the Greeks limited practice to a few, with political prognostications largely their bread and butter. Today, oracles are a widespread profession, few, besides pollsters, tied to politics, though it can certainly be argued the ambiguous drivel offered by professional pollsters has little political value. Most contemporary oracle guidance is tied to gaining wealth, such as economists and market analysts, who are more about predicting the future than offering any valuable perceptions on the present. Of course for any modern oracle, the past exists not at all.

Today, our greatest oracles are technologists. This is far and away the greatest difference between today and ancient times. Certainly, the Greeks had technology, though they didn't write about it much. It wasn't in any way as transformative as the industrial and now information technologies of the last two-centuries. The entire Classical Greek Era rose and declined as agricultural societies. Many tools, particularly those of war, changed from bronze to iron, but over the course of five centuries, daily life for most changed not terribly much. Change overwhelmingly was effected through war, political events, or natural crises such as earthquakes and droughts, thus the oracles' main concern of politics and the judgments of the gods.

In the last two-centuries, societal change has come overwhelmingly from technology, oddly, we remain anciently subjugated to the process. We venerate technologists looking to them as oracles of the future, instead of realizing the technology, not the person, is the only issue. We have no politics or political processes to deal with issues fostered by technology, such as how or even if we should develop any given technology, or accounting any given technology's long term impacts. We remain largely indifferent, as if it is out of our control, to how society deals with the impacts of technology in our daily lives or upon the greater environment.

Long assigned to history, Delphi remains instructive. We still rely on oracles. We remain largely in the Era of Oprah, politically disconnected individuals, atomized by technology into political impotence. Political value meaninglessly offered in the context of an archaic, broken system.

A democratic renaissance, Greek in nature, would include a politics of technology based not on divination, but education, discussion, participatory implementation, and whole environment accounting. It would require a much more complex participatory system providing continual feedback that can be simultaneously acted on. It would be an evolution of democratic politics, removing power from the prognostications of oracles and back to the hands of the people.

THE HUMAN USE OF HUMAN BEINGS

After publishing *Cybernetics* in 1948, Norbert Wiener wrote *The Human Use of Human Beings (1950)*. In the introduction he explains,

> "Upon the publication of this book (*Cybernetics*) which possesses a rather forbidding mathematical core, some of my friends urged upon me that I should write a related book for the layman, in which I should avoid mathematical symbolism and ideas as much as possible, and in which I should emphasize the not inconsiderable social consequences of my point of view."

He succeeds wonderfully, yet the book is unknown today, though it might well be considered the first rigorous thought on a politics of technology. It should be required reading for every high school student, so they can begin purposefully grappling with a society ever more greatly defined by technology. Finding this book made me wonder how at this time, it could remain completely unknown.

Wiener reasoned all learning involved the process of feedback, defined simplistically as any given initial system receiving information back from an action taken and then being able to incorporate that returned information, the feedback, into its next actions. "For any machine subject to a varied external environment, in order to act effectively it is necessary that information concerning the results of its own action be furnished to it as part of the information on which it must continue to act." He uses machine here, but feedback is just as essential to learning for any biological organism or for larger social systems comprising the two.

Wiener came to understand the essential role of feedback in his work developing anti-aircraft guns in World War II. Feedback in regards to the planes' velocities and the trajectory of the shells fired were necessary for calibrating and then recalibrating the guns' aim. Wiener knew the understanding of feedback and the development of the first computers signaled a new era of machine learning, of information systems allowing the automation not only of physical processes but of that most extremely nebulous conceptual process — intelligence. Wiener was gravely concerned the birth of this new technological era was directly tied to World War II, the greatest period of organized human violence in history. He courageously and correctly advocated not allowing militarism to lead the development of this evolving technological era precisely when the US institutionalized the National Security State, thus, the first reason Wiener disappeared.

In a 1947 letter to The Atlantic Magazine, Wiener warns,

"The measures taken during the war by our military agencies, in restricting the free intercourse among scientists on related projects or even on the same project, have gone so far that it is clear that if continued in time of peace this policy will lead to the total irresponsibility of the scientist, and ultimately to the death of science. Both of these are disastrous for our civilization, and entail grave and immediate peril for the public."

Wiener doubled down on the idiocy of allowing the military to lead technological development in *The Human Use of Human Beings:*

"However, it will not do for the masses of our scientific population to blame their appointed and self-appointed betters for their futility, and for the dangers of the present day. It is the great public which is demanding the utmost of secrecy for modern science in all things which may touch its military uses. This demand for secrecy is scarcely more than the wish of a sick civilization not to learn of the progress of its own disease. So long as we can continue to pretend that all is right with the world, we plug up our ears against the sound of 'Ancestral voices prophesying war.'"

Civilization only got sicker. The citizenry was ever more purposefully and blissfully ignorant of the actions of the American National Security as a primary force steering technological development, resulting in a continuous rain of death and destruction across the planet for the last 75 years – the latest examples Ukraine and Gaza.

However, there is a second not quite as barbarous reason for Wiener's anonymity, a more sophisticated marginalizing by an unaccountable, entrenched elite. This relegation to obscurity is well represented by a short piece published a decade ago by the MIT News, the university Wiener spent 40 years as a professor. The piece states,

> "Wiener's ideas ended up blending together with those of a number of his contemporaries to help create the intellectual backdrop against which engineering is done today. But it's difficult to isolate a single strain of thought in *Cybernetics* that had a lasting influence on subsequent scientific research."

"A single strain" is engineer think, but it goes much deeper. It is the tradition, blame Newton, of the compartmentalization of scientific thought since incorporated into the political, cultural, and economic structures of modern society. With political economy, Adam Smith defined it as "the division of labor," but it was preceded by the scientific division of intellect. Knowledge of a single strain of scientific thought proved immensely powerful in creating technology, which could then could be profitably exploited. Yet, political, cultural, and economic systems proved deaf, dumb, blind, and largely impenetrable to the feedback provided by adopted technologies' impact on the greater societal and environmental whole.

Wiener correctly advocated a more sophisticated and complex thinking, an understanding every division, every strain, remains part of a larger whole, and the action of any part influences the whole, while simultaneously the whole continuously influences actions of any given part. The ability of any specific entity, whether organic, machine, or a greater societal system for that matter, to receive feedback from actions taken and then incorporate this feedback into future actions is learning. The last century of technological development has incorporated little feedback, ignorantly proceeding with seemingly ever greater acceleration.

The MIT News piece adds "researchers in a host of disciplines drew inspiration from Wiener's syncretic vision." Wiener's math was foundational for developing present information technologies, his concepts essential for what is now being marketed as AI. The inability to value Wiener's thinking as a single strain meant the ideas could not be valued by established convention. *The Human Use of Human Beings* entire thesis is that valuing by dividing, through isolated, single, technological strains is an insufficient mean to measure the value of any new technology. Just as the technology being created would overthrow established society, the only way to truly value it was to eradicate the limited values creating it.

Today, we remain less aware of the need for a more sophisticated and encompassing, a more whole, valuing of technology than Wiener advocated in 1950. He writes a still spot-on critique of tech development,

"To those of us who are engaged in constructive research and in invention, there is a serious moral risk of aggrandizing what we have accomplished. To the public, there is an equally serious moral risk of supposing that in stating new potentials of fact, we scientists and engineers are thereby justifying and even urging their exploitation at any costs. It will therefore be taken for granted by many that the attitude of an investigator who is aware of the great new possibilities of the machine age, when employed for the purpose of communication and control, will be to urge the prompt exploitation of this new "know-how" for the sake of the machine and for the minimization of the human element in life. This is most emphatically not the purpose of the present book."

He then continues,

"That we shall have to change many details of our mode of life in the face of the new machines is certain; but these machines are secondary in all matters of value that concern us to the proper evaluation of human beings for their own sake and to their employment as human beings, and not as second-rate surrogates for possible machines of the future. The message of this book as well as its title is the human use of human beings."

Thus the third reason no one knows about Wiener, tech development has preceded apace not on its value to human beings, but simply valued by the technology itself. "It is again the American worship of know-how as opposed to know-what that hampers us."

Wiener's thought is a seismic shift in the understanding and shaping of both society's physical and social infrastructures, a reformation of value gained only through the concerted, deliberate, and comprehensive reorganization of human associations. It is a radical politics.

❧ 4 ❧

THE POLITICS OF
INFORMATION

OWNING THE SUN

Democracy in America is broken. In the interactions of the citizenry, you'd be hard pressed to demonstrate politics even exists. Outside an exceedingly small, increasingly zealous minority, most people can't be bothered. Proof of point is a simple one. When have you ever had a political discussion about or voted for a candidate based on their patent policy? This isn't a trick question. The answer is never, despite the question of patents being of essential importance for the political economy of the 20th century and even more fundamental to the 21st.

Into this political void drops Alexander Zaitchik's excellent history, *Owning the Sun: A People's History of Monopoly Medicine From Aspirin to COVID-19 Vaccines*. The book is a work of inestimable value regarding the pharmaceutical industry's rewriting and controlling the patent process for their own interests and unmitigated greed, neither of which are by any means exceptional.

Zaitchik covers many essential issues necessary for any sort of politics in the 21st century. Issues barely discussed publicly and completely absent from the marketing and advertising campaigns now sold as politics. *Owning the Sun* is a book about information—the lifeblood of politics—and the history of how patents became controlled exclusively by and for the benefit of a few.

Zaitchik documents the medical industry's long path from its beginnings, largely as a charitable public service, populated by a great many charlatans, to becoming one of the most formidable and profitable sectors of contemporary society, populated by charlatans of a different sort. In telling the drug industry's story, *Owning the Sun* reveals the change of America's democratic politics, most detrimentally, the abject failure of the republic's politics to keep up in almost every way with the changes brought about by the growth of scientific knowledge and its resulting technology.

Our traditions of the corporation and patent largely come out of the English monarchy. Ever since, this royal birth has continued shaping their development. The initial purpose of both allowed the monarchy to cede to another entity, for a limited time and purpose (literally Ltd.), economic power otherwise considered exclusively royal. "Monopolies," a term as closely associated with patents as corporations, were granted by the monarchy. It was a system quickly abused.

The English Parliament's 1642 "Statue of Monopolies" relieved the monarchy of some of this power, saying monopolies were, "'Contrary to the *lawes* of the *Realme*,' but followed an older Venetian law in allowing one significant carve-out. 'The true and first Inventor' of new modes of manufacture were eligible to receive a limited and exclusive grant to use and profit from their invention."

A little over a century later, after throwing off the British monarchy and establishing the US Constitution, Americans created a clause on patents. *Article I, Section 8, Clause 8* states, "To promote the progress of science and useful arts, by securing for limited times to authors and inventors the exclusive right to their respective writings and discoveries." It is basically the English monarchical understanding of patents claiming a monopoly for a limited time and purpose. However, in a more republican notion of promoting the general welfare, patents are founded not on an individual's right of profit, but "to promote the progress of science and useful arts."

The constitution's patent clause was by no means uncontroversial. Indeed the greatest democratic republicans of the founding pantheon thought patents unnecessary. Both Thomas Jefferson and Benjamin Franklin, both in every way the most quintessential Americans, opposed the idea of patents. One of the great figures of the 18th century, Franklin was a world renown scientist and inventor, publisher, successful businessman, and citizen. Zaitchik expounds Franklin's views on patents,

> "In his autobiography, Franklin explains his position through the story of an English ironmonger who made 'a little fortune' by patenting Franklin's published blueprints for a novel stove design. 'I declined [the patent] from a principle that has weighed with me on such occasions,' wrote Franklin, '*viz., that as we enjoy great advantages from the inventions of others, we should be glad of an opportunity to serve others by any invention of ours, and this we should do freely and generously.*' The italics are in the original, giving the advice the weight of maxim in his manual for right living."

Jefferson, who was Minister to France during the constitution's drafting, writes to James Madison, the constitution's architect, concerning the patent clause, "The benefits of these rights were 'too doubtful to be opposed to that of their general suppression.'" In a wise aphorism about knowledge and information, Jefferson writes, "He who receives an idea from me, receives instruction himself without lessening mine; as he who lights his taper at mine, receives light without darkening me."

Franklin's and Jefferson's views are those of democratic republicans, an understanding on the importance of the freedom of information, knowledge, and its utilization foremost for the general welfare. It is a fundamental difference to a monarchical system's granting of patents, as something done in limited scope, a cautious, temporary bestowing of what by right is something belonging exclusively to the sovereign. In the 19th and 20th centuries, Jefferson's and Franklin's republican patent notions were turned completely on their head. Patents became exclu-

sive levers of power used first and foremost for the benefit of industry's new monarchical institution – the corporation.

With the rise of industry, and its seminal social invention, the
corporation, patents proliferated across 19th century America, increasingly bestowed with the legal value of property. Ironically, just as slavery, that other peculiar institution of property met its demise,
knowledge was increasingly enslaved. By the end of the 19th century,
limiting the growing power of the new industrial corporation became a
political issue popularly known as antitrust, an issue of power eventually decided entirely in favor of the corporation. Zaitchik astutely
points out, "Of the two landmark bills passed in response to rising
antitrust sentiment—the Interstate Commerce Act of 1887 and the
Sherman Act of 1890—both remained mute on the subject of patents."

Instead of in any way subjecting or even balancing the growing
power of the corporation, government, most especially the Supreme
Court became their handmaidens. With an intimate understanding of
the power of patents, corporations became patent factories.

"The nineteenth-century names most associated with the
legend of the individual genius—Edison, Morse, Goodyear,
Westinghouse, Ford—were in fact its most prominent gravedig-
gers. They built research castles and pulled the drawbridge,
forcing those who might wish to follow them to overcome
rising financial and legal barriers maintained by teams of in-
house corporate patent lawyers."

Alexander Graham Bell was especially notorious for spouting
extensive public relations about the heroic lone inventor, while simultaneously running a patent assembly line. The Supreme Court
bestowed legal justification;

"The last of several Bell decisions in 1897 testified to the
distance that now separated U.S. law from the social contract
that had defined the grand patent bargain for a thousand years.
'The inventor is one who has discovered something of value,'

wrote the majority in United States v. American Bell Telephone Co. 'It is his absolute property. He may withhold the knowledge of it from the public.'"

Not exactly the sentiments of *Section 1, Article 8, Clause 8,* where patents promote "the progress of science and useful arts." Instead, a ruling better understood as a restoration of monarchical power. From this mess emerges modern medicine.

Well into the 20th century, medicine was largely synonymous with charity, a public good, many of its largest institutions run by religious orders. Zaitchik writes at its "founding convention in Philadelphia in 1847, the forerunner of the American Medical Association (AMA) adopted a code of ethics declaring patents 'incompatible with the duty and obligation enjoined upon physicians to advance the knowledge of curing diseases.'"

"Medical and pharmaceutical guilds were allied in a 'profound belief in their own supposed benevolence and dedication to the advancement of scientific knowledge,' writes Joseph M. Gabriel, the preeminent historian of nineteenth-century American medical ethics and mores. 'For most physicians, there was little difference between patenting and secrecy when it came to drugs. Both were considered unethical forms of selfish monopoly. Indeed, it was generally assumed that patented remedies and quack nostrums were the same thing.'"

For most of the 19th century, "patent" medicines were associated with the miracle cures and snake oils peddled by assorted shameless charlatans. This would change by the end of the century. The Germans were the largest initial force industrializing medicine, no company more responsible than *Farbenfabriken vormals Friedrich Bayer*, known in the US simply as Bayer. With their development and patenting of a number of drugs, including heroin, but most essentially Aspirin (the brand name), Bayer began reconfiguring medicine, most specifically the burgeoning pharmaceutical industry.

Over the next fifty years, medicine's once charitable association faded, profit became defining. By the middle of the century,

"The taboo against medical monopolies had turned into a race to collect and defend, by hook or by crook, the seventeen-year patents that had become the coin of the pharmaceutical realm. The huge markups these patents enabled made U.S. drug prices the highest in the world, producing corporate profit margins unique to the postwar economy, double and often triple those found in other manufacturing sectors."

Zaitchik continues,

"U.S. drug firms introduced, on average, fifty new products every year during the 1950s—twice the rate of the previous decade. But these blockbuster drugs were marketed under a profusion of pricey trademarks through advertising campaigns designed to push pills in ways once associated with "patent-medicines" of the previous century."

Zaitchik tells the essential history of the first half of 20th century American politics wrestling with the questions of corporate and patent powers. He lays out, though doesn't quite completely tie together how American politics changed in this process, democracy in America crushed.

Owning the Sun is a history of centralizing economic power under the industrial corporation and the resulting reactionary forwarding of centralized political power in Washington DC. The greatest movement occurred in a relatively short time with the New Deal. This isn't a nefarious condemnation of the New Deal. The New Deal was largely a good faith reaction to the collapse of the national economy that had evolved with American industrialization over the previous century. Sincere and well meaning individuals sought in every way to revive and regulate this system. However, few, Supreme Court Justice Louis Brandeis being one major exception, looked at the longer term problems this great centralization of political power in DC would cause the republic.

In 1943, a century after its birth, the AMA, along with every other industry association, opened an office in DC. Patents were only one information currency, there was also the currency of politics itself, both amongst the citizenry and in the legislatures. The politics of the citizenry gradually became truncated entirely into biennial or quadrennial elections. Increasingly, apolitical campaigns, nothing more than marketing and advertising exercises for an array of faulty products, were entirely dominated and funded by the concentrated wealth created through corporate power.

The debasement of the legislative process was just as obscene. It was impossible for an institution like the Congress with only 535 people and some thousands of staff to in any way deal with the complexities and tsunami of information produced by 20th century industrial society. This need was met with the birth of the lobbying industry, think-tanks, public relations, etc., comprised of the corporations themselves or their funded associations. They framed the debate on issues and eventually wrote the legislation.

In the 1950's, out of history's greatest monopolist John D Rockefeller's University of Chicago came corporate handbooks on how to deal with regulation. An important figure in this effort was economist George Stigler.

"Stigler and those influenced by his work had very sophisticated ideas about how to audit and slowly take over the agencies by getting them to internalize [their] positions and critiques. You target public conceptions of medical science. You target the agencies' understanding of what they're supposed to do. You target the very thing inputted into the regulatory bodies—you commercialize science. Outside of Chicago, Stigler, his students, and those in their close orbit developed relationships with scientists, resulting in a variety of interlinked and coordinated research institutes spanning economics, politics, and the biomedical sciences."

Combined with control of the election process, calling this system democratic would be a stretch. Zaitchik documents several unsuccessful attempts of the old republic to fight back and hang on. Anachronistic legislators such as the old populist West Virginia Senator Kilgore and his protégé Tennessee Senator Estes Kefauver's, single-handedly attempt to fight the corporate patent oligarchy, a patent process amusingly enough funded extensively with public dollars. At the start of his 1957 hearing on patents Kefauver warns, "It is only a step from the loss of economic freedom to the loss of political freedom."

With the dawn of a new, even more radical information era, the Supreme Court once again lays down the law of who will be in control. In 1980, "A 5–4 decision written by Warren Burger, the Court overruled the U.S. Patent Office and ruled that codified genes were patentable, as was 'anything under the sun that is made by man.'"

The book's final chapters come from today's COVID-19 headlines. Out of the computer industry and into the medical industry steps experienced information mogul, former Microsoft Chairman Bill Gates, greedily looking to add to his already formidable billions. Gates understands better than most the power of controlling information. Walking into the vaccine business he brings,

> "Richard Wilder, a former head of intellectual property at Microsoft who serves as general counsel and director of business development at Gates's flagship infectious disease research initiative, the Coalition for Epidemic Preparedness Innovations (CEPI)."

Phew, MS-HEALTH! One has to ask what's the CTRL-ALT-DEL, the reboot function, when the whole system crashes?

Gates' influence and insistence on intellectual property controls helped hamstring the COVID vaccine roll out, especially in the global south. "In February 2021, 75 percent of all existing vaccines had been administered in just ten countries. On the other side of these 130 million doses, close to 130 countries containing 2.5 billion people had yet to administer a single shot." As we've come to learn with the virus' endless mutations, viruses don't much care about intellectual property.

The South Africans, well familiar with imperious white boys attempting to run the show exclusively for their own benefit in the name of the greater public good, issued a stinging rebuke to the Gates' led COVAX vaccine distribution effort. The South Africans hammer,

> "Rather large gap exists between what COVAX can deliver and what is required in developing and least developed countries. Irrespective of the amount of money any of the donor countries may throw at the problem, the model of donation and philanthropic expediency cannot solve the fundamental disconnect between the monopolistic model it underwrites and the very real desire of developing and least developed countries to produce for themselves. Philanthropy cannot buy equality. The artificial shortage of vaccines is primarily caused by the inappropriate use of intellectual property rights; this cannot be allowed to continue."

"Philanthropy cannot buy equality." What a wonderfully astute essential democratic understanding! A fundamental democratic tenet once widely understood in an America of another era. An essential principle of the long fight against concentrating economic power, which largely makes philanthropy necessary in the first place.

Zaitchik concludes of the present pharmaceutical industry,

> "By the standards of any civilization that views its medicines as crowning achievements, the regime that prices them beyond reach and restricts the knowledge to make them must be, and has been, ruled a failure."

The book's title, *Owning the Sun* comes from polio vaccine creator Jonas Salk. Polio had been a scourge for decades, particularly impacting children. When announcing the vaccine, Salk was asked if he would patent it. He replied, "Could you patent the sun?" Maybe not, but in the words of Supreme Court Justice Burger, it appears you can patent everything under the sun.

The most ironic thing about all this is that the limited times antitrust was decisively used over the last century, the results have had undeniable economic and public benefits. The breaking up of Standard Oil created seven companies of combined value greater than the established monopoly. The post-war release of the patents controlled by aluminum manufacturer Alcoa were great assets to the metals' industry as a whole. Forcing Bell Labs to license their patents created the entire contemporary electronics industry. AT&T's breakup helped bring about the internet's mass adoption. While stopping Microsoft's takeover of the internet, well, it created a few other big companies of dubious value. Unfortunately, it could be argued MS may have just as well and probably more atrociously created the present internet cesspool.

There is absolutely no economic argument against an exponentially more public patent process, while the political argument to break up these mega-corporations is irrefutable, if you want democracy anyway.

Owning the Sun is a masterful history of the politics of information. Compared to previous human history, industrialism required massive amounts of information, its control proved defining in every way. As a new technological era spills forth, information is even more fundamental and ubiquitous. Presently, the world lacks the politics, institutions, and thought to in any way constructively engage this challenge.

WIENER & SHANNON: TOWARD A POLITICS OF INFORMATION

A couple decades ago, the term "Information Age" was bandied about to define our new technological era, not so much anymore. Maybe, unlikely as it appears, we realize we remain firmly entrenched in industrialism and we've never really understood that. Claiming the era was the Information Age was never quite right. From our beginnings, information has been an integral, one can say an essential defining component of *Homo sapiens*. From the oldest culture, the ability to control fire, tilling the soil, and the relatively recent invention of the printing press, information has been an intrinsic feature of humanity. With the invention of electric media followed by the networked microprocessor, humanity's dependence on information increased exponentially. Today, our inability to effectively utilize both the quantity and quality of information overwhelms our established economic, cultural and government institutions. In order to understand this deluge of information and to in any way provide qualitative measures of value, we need a politics of information.

What precisely is information? This is a question still difficult to answer. There isn't a simple answer. We might borrow American Supreme Court Justice Potter Stewart's line about defining pornography, "I know it when I see it." From the original Latin, *sapiens* could be defined as "thinking," the popular connotation of "wise" is a little bit of stretch when preceded by *Homo.* Thinking implies information, whether provided by the senses or abstractly generated in our minds.

In 1948, at the dawn of the age of the transistor, two essential books about information were published. One was Claude Shannon's *The Mathematical Theory of Communication,* the second, Norbert Wiener's, *Cybernetics or Control and Communication in the Animal and the Machine.* As seen from the titles, both focus on communication, neither provide a strict or simple answer to what is information. In fact, in his wonderful introduction to Shannon's work, mathematician Warren Weaver writes,

"The concept of information developed in this theory at first seems disappointing and bizarre - disappointing because it has nothing to do with meaning, and bizarre because it deals not with a single message but rather with the statistical character of a whole ensemble of messages, bizarre also because in these statistical terms the two words information and uncertainty find themselves to be partners."

Despite this uncertainty and the inherent contradiction of concept, both works have been essential to providing the thought and math upon which the computer industry and resulting communication infrastructures have been built. It's by no means extraordinary that so much has been accomplished with information without a definition of what exactly it is. After all, no one can tell you what gravity is. We understand it by dropping an object, watching tides, or calculating the planets' paths around the sun. Similarly, energy and matter are known more by their characteristics and actions than any precise definition of what exactly they are. What all three have in common, starting with Galileo's and Newton's equations, is with ever more sophisticated mathematics, we have been able to create ever more sophisticated technologies to manipulate mass, energy, and information.

However, turning to Wiener's thought at the top of this paper, it is essential to understand information is not energy or matter. Begun ten-thousand years ago, we can look at the Agrarian Era as a leap in our abilities to manipulate matter. The Industrial Age, only several centuries old, is overwhelmingly shaped by our ability to manipulate mass quantities of energy. Wiener writes the difference between industrial and information technologies "as the distinction between power and communication engineering. It is this split which separates the age just past from that in which we are now living." While industrialism is dependent on information, it is defined by the harnessing of vast quantities of energy. While the technologies developed over the past 75 years are predominately defined by their ability to manipulate information, but entirely dependent on energy.

Both Shannon's and Wiener's theory reveal that understanding information is inherently bound with its communication. Shannon's book focuses on the process of communication, how information is carried by a message comprised of signals. It focuses on a linear, a simple communication system architecture, that begins with a source and ends with the receiver, input matches output in sum and shape. Shannon provides a sophisticated math for this system that led to the creation of ever more sophisticated communication gadgets, most especially our digital systems consisting of computers and their now ubiquitous networks.

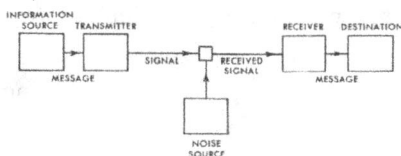

Fig. 1. — Schematic diagram of a general communication system.

From Shannon's Theory of Communication

In Weaver's introduction to Shannon's work, he breaks down communication theory into three parts:

LEVEL A. How accurately can the symbols of communication be transmitted? (The technical problem.)

LEVEL B. How precisely do the transmitted symbols convey the desired meaning? (The semantic problem.)

LEVEL C. How effectively does the received meaning affect conduct in the desired way? (The effectiveness problem.)

Weaver then writes,

"The word information, in this theory, is used in a special sense that must not be confused with its ordinary usage. In particular, information must not be confused with meaning. In fact, two messages, one of which is heavily loaded with meaning and the other of which is pure nonsense, can be exactly equivalent, from the present viewpoint, as regards information. It is this, undoubtedly, that Shannon means when he says that 'the semantic aspects of communication are irrelevant to the engineering aspects.'"

Attempting to provide any rigor to the term "ordinary usage," we fairly quickly find any definition of information rather nebulous.

What's imperative to understand with Shannon's work, it doesn't deal with information's meaning. Information is defined through its communication, the engineering aspect of getting a message transmitted from source to receiver

In regards to Weaver's three part outline of communications theory, Shannon's work only concerns Level A ,"the technical problem." However, Weaver adds, "But this does not mean that the engineering aspects are necessarily irrelevant to the semantic aspects." Inherent in any communication technology we use, the medium shapes information both in its transmission and its reception in certain ways that can be as important as the information itself. A decade later, this was brilliantly expressed by technology historian Marshall McLuhan with, "The medium is the message."

This might simply be recognized by the differences in our senses, which are information collectors, yet the variety of engineering behind sight, hearing, smell, and touch are all essential to understanding the information received.

In some ways, Wiener's *Cybernetics* is more essential to the present and future, most especially for constructing a politics of information. Wiener's work is more encompassing, rooted in historical and political context, not just simply the operation of technology from the insights of engineering, but how it comes to be and grappling with the greater societal implications. As Wiener's astutely comments, an acute criticism that could be applied to the then just forming Tech industry, "I know very great engineers who never think further than the construction of the gadget and never think of the question of the integration of the gadget with human beings in the society."

Most importantly, Wiener's insights differ from Shannon's in that he looks at not just one direction communication, but how messages are sent and then returned, which necessitates a greater understanding of whatever larger organization the communication system is embedded. *Cybernetics* looks not simply at Weaver's Level A communication, but requires an understanding of both Levels B, the information's meaning, and C, its impact on the receiver. Key to this understanding is feedback, simply understood as when a source emits a message, what message is returned in response. Feedback is "centered not around the

technique of electrical engineering but around the much more fundamental notion of the message, whether this should be transmitted by
electrical, mechanical, or nervous means." Feedback provides a more
rigorous, though by no means comprehensive understanding of information. It places the communication system into larger context in that
it concerns how a mechanical or organic entity operates autonomously.

Just as with Shannon's work, Wiener's insights are largely mathematical constructs, feedback "is a phenomenon which we understand
very thoroughly from a quantitative point of view." Most importantly,
the math underneath both theories is the statistical math used to
provide the insights of quantum mechanics. The theories "belong to
the Gibbsian statistical mechanics rather than to the classical
Newtonian mechanics."

Weaver notes on Shannon's theory,

"In doing this, we have made of communication engineering
design a statistical science, a branch of statistical mechanics. ...
The notion of the amount of information attaches itself very
naturally to a classical notion in statistical mechanics: that of
entropy. Just as the amount of information in a system is a
measure of its degree of organization, so the entropy of a
system is a measure of its degree of disorganization; and the
one is simply the negative of the other."

This fundamentally probabilistic, uncertain, and relative world, is
completely ignored in the proclamations and evangelizing of our technological determinists. Wiener states, "In quantum mechanics, the
whole past of an individual system does not determine the future of
that system in any absolute way but merely the distribution of possible
futures of the system." Essentially adding, "In general, there is no set
of observations conceivable which can give us enough information
about the past of a system to give us complete information as to its
future."

This understanding is imperative to understanding the development of technology, the unacknowledged degree of randomness
involved, or in looking at politically, the amount of choice or who

chooses. Instead, the history of established technologies are written as if their existence and adoption were always pre-determined, maybe some underlying Calvinistic predestination accounts for this mindset, though it's not surprising given these histories largely emanate from power structures the technologies themselves created. Worse, our last half-century "Tech" era haphazardly or more accurately hazardously, indiscriminately bestows labels like visionary to technologists, yet it is a process overwhelmingly shaped today, as Wiener astutely described in a 1950 talk as "extremely tempting to anybody who wants to make a quick fortune and leave the rest of the community to try and pick up the pieces."

Wiener sets our contemporary technological revolution in an historical frame,

> "Perhaps I may clarify the historical background of the present situation if I say that the first industrial revolution, the revolution of the "dark satanic mills," was the devaluation of the human arm by the competition of machinery. There is no rate of pay at which a United States pick-and-shovel laborer can live which is low enough to compete with the work of a steam shovel as an excavator."

He then concludes, computers, the latest generation promoted as AI (Artificial Intelligence) are,

> "Similarly bound to devalue the human brain, at least in its simpler and more routine decisions. ...taking the second revolution as accomplished, the average human being of mediocre attainments or less has nothing to sell that is worth anyone's money to buy. The answer, of course, is to have a society based on human values other than buying or selling. To arrive at this society, we need a good deal of planning and a good deal of struggle, which, if the best comes to the best, may be on the plane of ideas, and otherwise—who knows?"

In short, Wiener describes the necessity for a politics of technology, first with industrial technologies shaped by mass energy usage and then our new communication technologies dependent on information. A politics of industrial technology remains to this day little understood, barely formed, the politics of information, nonexistent.

Wiener's conclusions on the need for a politics of technology seven decades ago are just as relevant today:

> "It gives the human race a new and most effective collection of mechanical slaves to perform its labor. Such mechanical labor has most of the economic properties of slave labor, although, unlike slave labor, it does not involve the direct demoralizing effects of human cruelty. However, any labor that accepts the conditions of competition with slave labor accepts the conditions of slave labor, and is essentially slave labor. The key word of this statement is competition. It may very well be a good thing for humanity to have the machine remove from it the need of menial and disagreeable tasks, or it may not. I do not know. It cannot be good for these new potentialities to be assessed in the terms of the market, of the money they save; and it is precisely the terms of the open market, the "fifth freedom," that have become the shibboleth of the sector of American opinion represented by the National Association of Manufacturers and the Saturday Evening Post. I say American opinion, for as an American, I know it best, but the hucksters recognize no national boundary."

The processes we euphemistically and unhelpfully call markets are not simply at this point problematic, but become ever greatly more insufficient to in any way healthily guide technological development. Even more incapable of guiding us are our archaic agrarian government structures and a completely dysfunctional political system. If we are to "have a society based on human values other than buying or selling" these processes, systems, and institutions must be radically reformed.

From our days of hunting and gathering, politics has been a communication process. Politics is fundamentally an information system. Both Wiener's and Shannon's insights offer conceptual and process analogies on how we might reform our politics, government, and economy. We can begin with Wiener's ideas on feedback, the communication necessary for any autonomous system. Feedback creates "intelligence," systems that dynamically adjust, such systems Wiener called "cybernetic."

He writes,

"The entire field of control and communication theory, whether in the machine or in the animal, by the name Cybernetics, which we form from the Greek χυβερνήτης or steersman. In choosing this term, we wish to recognize that the first significant paper on feedback mechanisms is an article on governors, which was published by Clerk Maxwell in 1868, and that governor is derived from a Latin corruption of χυβερνήτης. We also wish to refer to the fact that the steering engines of a ship are indeed one of the earliest and best-developed forms of feedback mechanisms."

All social systems are organized through communication, feedback plays an essential role. Indeed, Wiener writes, "The community extends only so far as there extends an effectual transmission of information." In certain respects the role of government has always been similar to a mechanical governor, providing a mechanism for control and order through adjustment.

Wiener writes,

"It is certainly true that the social system is an organization like the individual, that it is bound together by a system of communication, and that it has a dynamics in which circular processes of a feedback nature play an important part."

Yet, with our politics, here I use politics' most encompassing definition, – how society structures and determines life – feedback mechanisms are completely broken, whether looked at from a cultural, economic, technological, or environmental perspective.

Every political system has feedback mechanisms providing stability.

THE POLITICS OF APE AND MACHINE

It's somewhat misconstrued that hierarchical systems of governance, such as monarchies or other despotic regimes, were simply top-down. No centralized hierarchical system lasted long that had no effective feedback coming from the bottom back to the top. As a communication channel, the channel from the top to the bottom was much wider than the one coming back from the bottom to the top. But no centralized system, no matter how brutal, lasted long without feedback from the bottom and some corresponding response from the top.

Centralized power can be looked at as linear, "the simplest control systems are linear," as opposed to more complex, non-linear systems, such as ourselves and all other biological organisms. Wiener writes about our just beginning understanding of the human body,

> "A complex additive system like this cannot be stabilized by a single feedback. ...In short, our inner economy must contain an assembly of thermostats, automatic controls, governors, and the like, which would be adequate for a great chemical plant. These are what we know collectively as our homeostatic mechanism."

Homeostasis in complex organisms is gained by numerous processes providing stability to the whole. They involve any number of actions flowing from an initial state which in turn are met by information returned from the resulting initial action — feedback. These continual actions and reactions provide a relative equilibrium helping keep the system stable. An easy example in the human body is temperature control, where innumerable processes produce and consume energy, yet the entire body remains at a constant temperature.

Centralized hierarchical systems of government are uncomplex, a limited number of concentrated systems of control receiving limited feedback necessary for homeostasis. Stability is controlled or attempts to be controlled by the top. At the other end of the political spectrum is democracy, control is more distributed, actions continuously, distributedly instigated, feedback returned from numerous sources. This constant, complex interaction provides systemic stability – homeostasis.

In looking at modern republicanism, particularly the American system, its founding saw a highly distributed system of local, state, and federal governments, atop a predominately agrarian economy comprised largely of small farms. In the course of two and half centuries, the agrarian economy was transformed into an industrial economy. Economic power became increasingly centralized in ever more massive corporations, while government power progressively centralized in DC.

Traditional political communication was also centralized. The invention and implementation of broadcast media overwhelmed the more traditionally distributed newspapers, local political parties and associations mostly disappeared. Feedback, once largely provided in person, became more and more dominated by crude polling samples. Marketing and advertising crafted from these polling samples was then pushed back across centralized media to mass audiences. We are told, or more accurately sold, the internet's ability to more personalize this process is some sort of advance. Regarding government, the citizenry had no direct input to the system, no feedback, except for every two years on election day. Political communication, once complex and non-linear, became increasingly linear. Democratic action atrophied, politics grew ever more dysfunctional.

Wiener astutely accessed the situation growing in America,

"It is only in the large community, where the Lords of Things as They Are protect themselves from hunger by wealth, from public opinion by privacy and anonymity, from private criticism by the laws of libel and the possession of the means of communication, that ruthlessness can reach its most sublime levels. Of all of these anti-homeostatic factors in society, the control of the means of communication is the most effective and most important."

Adding,

"In a society like ours, avowedly based on buying and selling, in which all natural and human resources are regarded as the absolute property of the first business man enterprising enough to exploit them, these secondary aspects of the means of communication tend to encroach further and further on the primary ones."

There are two very important things to understand from the above statements. The first is that information, beyond simple quantitative communication, needs context to in any way be valuable. In Weaver's three components of communication theory this concerns levels B and C, how information is interpreted and then how useful it becomes. Today, at a societal level, context is overwhelmingly provided by massive established forces, monopolist corporations and centralized government institutions – "the Lords of Things as They Are," more powerful today than when Wiener first labeled them.

Wiener correctly foresaw information technologies increasing exponentially, thus too the quantity of information. Along with this growth in the quantity of information, just as importantly grew the quantity of "noise," the other essential component of information theory – Uncertainty, Weaver's information partner. In his introduction to Shannon, Weaver provides a simple definition of noise as, "In the process of being transmitted, it is unfortunately characteristic that certain things are added to the signal which were not intended by the information source." Now it gets a little tricky here understanding the use of statistical math as the basis of information theory, especially confusing in regards to the many ways we traditionally conceive and experience the daily workings of our everyday world.

Weaver writes,

"How does noise affect information? Information is, we must steadily remember (in Shannon's theory), a measure of one's freedom of choice in selecting a message. The greater this freedom of choice, and hence the greater the information, the greater is the uncertainty that the message actually selected is some particular one. Thus greater freedom of choice, greater uncertainty, greater information go hand in hand."

Weaver helpfully adds, "Uncertainty which arises by virtue of freedom of choice on the part of the sender is desirable uncertainty. Uncertainty which arises because of errors or because of the influence of noise is undesirable uncertainty."

In regards to how we traditionally define politics, the rapid rise of the internet and resulting explosion of information has created massive political noise, straining and increasingly undermining established democratic structures, giving ever greater power to "the Lords of Things as They Are." Without an ability to complexly interact, that is to democratically choose, society's information tsunami creates ever greater uncertainty, an undesirable uncertainty with political messaging becoming ever greater noise.

This political noise consists of two separate though correlated parts. First is the inability to correctly interpret, to choose and act on information, what Weaver defines as Levels B and C of communication. Secondly, with the sheer quantity of information

"error and confusion arise and fidelity decreases, when, no matter how good the coding, one tries to crowd too much over a channel. Here again a general theory at all levels will surely have to take into account not only the capacity of the channel but also (even the words are right!) the capacity of the audience. If one tries to overcrowd the capacity of the audience, it is probably true, by direct analogy, that you do not, so to speak, fill the audience up and then waste only the remainder by spilling. More likely, and again by direct analogy, if you overcrowd the capacity of the audience you force a general and inescapable error and confusion." (Weaver)

Industrialization and the rise of broadcast media produced a massive rise in the quantity of information. Over the last century, in response to this communication problem, as the quantity of information grew and political power became more centralized, statistical analysis became prominent as an attempt to deal with the information onslaught.

However, Wiener warned this statistical analysis would prove inadequate, that "the main quantities affecting society are not only statistical, but the runs of statistics on which they are based are excessively short. For a good statistic of society, we need long runs under essentially constant conditions." Which we didn't have then and don't have now, most especially in this era of incessant technological churning, where the society of today differs vastly from yesterday and even more so from tomorrow. He concludes, "Thus the human sciences are very poor testing-grounds for a new mathematical technique."

But that certainly didn't stop "the Lords of Things as They Are," in fact they desperately searched their statistics with ever greater intensity looking for answers that aren't there. Our academic, government, and corporate institutions spew unending statistics in defense of failing policies. Wiener concludes, "There is much which we must leave, whether we like it or not, to the un-'scientific,' narrative method of the professional historian." Unfortunately, the one thing entirely lost to our technology saturated, information inundated society is all historical understanding. History still offers a foundation to help navigate our technological future. I speak here not merely of human history, but the natural history from which *Homo sapiens* were conceived.

The great question is how we restructure society, our processes and institutions, to better transmit, measure, and value information. Shannon stated, "Frequently the messages have meaning; that is they refer to or are correlated according to some system with certain physical or conceptual entities. These semantic aspects of communication are irrelevant to the engineering problem." Yet, in the introduction, where Weaver lays out the three components of communication theory, he correctly notes that the architecture does indeed at times impact the meaning, the semantics. The system's architecture, its engineering, in part "overlaps" the meaning, "more than one could possibly naively suspect."

This understanding is politically imperative, simply, the democratic processing of information is only possible with a democratic architecture, a democratic engineering of information systems. In the simple linear communication system schematic at the top of this piece, Weaver imagines "another box labeled 'Semantic Receiver' interposed between the engineering receiver (which changes signals to messages) and the destination." Politically, this should be the main job of associations, organizations of people producing, editing, and interpreting, providing meaning and context to information. Politically, there is a need to create distributed networked systems with innumerable channels connecting multitudes of associations of individuals choosing to act on any given information, simultaneously providing feedback across the networks.

Again going back to the inherent statistical and probabilistic nature of information theory, communication has a direct definitional relation to entropy. A message can be pulled out of a larger ocean of "noise" simply by its order in relation to the greater disorder it is ensconced. Weaver writes,

> "In doing this, we have made communication engineering design a statistical science, a branch of statistical mechanics. ...The notion of the amount of information attaches itself very naturally to a classical notion in statistical mechanics: that of entropy. Just as the amount of information in a system is a measure of its degree of organization, so the entropy of a system is a measure of its degree of disorganization; and the one is simply the negative of the other."

Just as with quantum physics and Darwinian evolution, information's meaning is partly subjective, relative, derived in relation to its greater environment. This idea of subjectivity is in direct opposition to Plato's notion of forms, that is of single objective meaning. This idea of objectivity goes even further back than the Greeks, inherent in the idea of centralized government, of concentrated control, and immutable laws. Of course it was never true these systems were objective, just the opposite. Meaning was first and foremost provided in defense of the centralized system of power. Information was controlled, edited, and communicated to insure the position and continuation of established power, objectivity was a means of power.

From an information system perspective, centralization is failing, statistics as means of governing are insufficient and imprecise measures leading to false values. Social systems are not linear systems, they are nonlinear, the information input in no way equals what's received, and just as importantly the seeming homogeneity of any given message can be interpreted in countless different ways.

With our contemporary centralized powers, the notion of information objectivity still strives, especially in the American National Security State and our leviathan corporations. It is accompanied and justified by, as with all despotic regimes of the past, a growing crippling dependence on secrecy haunting both sectors. At the dawning of the National Security State, Wiener summed up the problem in a 1950 talk as a "creeping paralysis of secrecy which is engulfing our government, secrecy simply means we are unable to face situations as they are, the people who have to control situations are in no position to handle them."

People in control of situations in no position to handle them. What better can describe America's dysfunction?

Democratically, we must embrace the flood of information, openness of communication, and the resulting subjectivity. Weaver points to the thought of the great physicist and astronomer Arthur Eddington,

"Suppose that we were asked to arrange the following in two categories - distance, mass, electric force, entropy, beauty, melody. I think there are the strongest grounds for placing entropy alongside beauty and melody, and not with the first three. Entropy is only found when the parts are viewed in association, and it is by viewing or hearing the parts in association that beauty and melody are discerned. All three are features of arrangement."

"Viewed in association," meaning provided relative to "arrangement." Again at the heart of many of our political problems is organizational ineptitude, a problem completely ignored by almost all political analysis.

We require understanding of the fundamental necessity of information creation, editing, and communication, as inherently political processes. Doing so requires the creation of innumerable associations, whether independent or essential components of every societal entity, an understanding of the necessity of "semantic receivers." As semantic receivers, such associations are advocates of subjective interpretations of information allowing choice in how it may be implemented. It should be noted regarding the recent popularity of "Artificial Intelligence," in the end, any computer's results will be subjective arising both from the information inputted and the very physical mechanisms of the computer itself. Centralized compute power is no more objective than an old sultan's palace.

Creating a political system that is information rich, distributedly networked, constantly interacting, and democratically subjective, requires much more organic processes. Systems more in common with biological complexity than the mechanical power of industrialism. After two centuries of industrialism, biology must reassert itself with an understanding all life flourishes in relation to its greater environment. We need to be reactionary in reasserting locality, creating associations that first and foremost seek to take advantage of their local geography, climate, and diversity of ecological systems, simultaneously interacting and creating the greater whole, as opposed to being homogenized and controlled from above.

We can structure society and our interactions with the greater environment by embracing the thing which makes us most human, sapiens. We can move from industrial values where society is designed by gross energy usage and instead use information to become more energy sophisticated, a return to being more defined by the greater environment, not simply through its manipulation using ever greater force.

From a biological, life systems perspective, it also means overturning long established ideas behind governance, most especially the idea that laws are meant for the ages. We need to look at laws as communication changing with feedback, interpretation varies as interaction provides definition, meaning evolves. We, every individual, are the equal components of an intricately complex information system, the body politic. It is a system that must literally come alive through continuous participation, our cultural, economic, and political inter-connections providing democratic homeostasis.

INFORMATION AND ENERGY

In 2022, Caleb Scharf authored a book, *The Ascent of Information: Books, Bits, Genes, Machines, and Life's Unending Algorithm,* perfectly illustrating an important contemporary conundrum: specialized technologies quickly derived from new scientific insights lack much of the under-lying science's larger understandings. This creates significant issues concerning technology's greater societal impacts. Questions rising from these developments in regards to all recent technologies remain essentially unexamined. Which isn't surprising, the same thing can still be said for centuries-old industrial technology.

The book valuably brings together various disciplines involved in the creation of the new world of information technology. However, the author's attempt to tie them all together under one grand information theory is flawed and unhelpful to any better understanding. There's an old joke started with Einstein's later life efforts to unite the various theories of 20th century physics. It goes, "Old physicists never die, they just try to create a unified field theory." Such is this book's great fault, but it still has important specific perspectives.

What is information? That's a very difficult question to answer. In many ways, information can only be defined within the context of how it is used, though defining through specific context clouds the ability to gain greater meaning.

Maybe defining information is a quandary best understood with the great physicist Niels Bohr's idea of complementarity. This idea is helpful for any "whole understanding" of quanta, and Bohr argued life in general. Understanding a single characteristic of any one object can only truly be understood in relation to every other characteristic, even if they are in direct contradiction. For example, characteristics of quanta such as light and electrons to be fully understood, must be looked at as both a particle and a wave. How you look defines what you find.

Or moving above the quantum world to human life, complementarity is valuable in understanding war. The only way to understand a war's beginnings, movements, and consequences is to understand the histories, thinking, and actions of all opposing sides.

With information, the harder, the more specific any given applied definition, in many ways excludes larger meaning. It can be argued, especially after reading Scharf's book, best to keep any general definition of information soft. Hard definitions are all tied to applied context – color, shape, quantity, a bear, a mouse, a word, a number – all are contextually information specific. All need larger context to be truly useful. Massive amounts of specialized information devoid of larger context is one of the great challenges facing science, technological development, and society as a whole.

The most valuable part of this book is tying together energy and information. Scharf is not the first to do this. The whole school of mid-20th century Information Theory developed by Claude Shannon, John Von Neuman, and others uses math concepts developed by physics to look at information as physics looks at energy. This way of manipulating information is the foundation of our present information technologies. It is undeniably powerful, but its specificity – specialized manipulation of innumerable calculable binary choices contextualized by the use of algorithms – prejudices any greater information environment. As a whole, life is neither constrained by binary choices or defined by algorithms.

In a physics's understanding of information, there's an intriguing and essential view of the anti-entropy value of information. Scharf writes, "Informational entropy and physical entropy are two inextricably linked sides to the same story." Entropy outside its very specific thermodynamic meaning is a soft and often greatly misused concept. In thermodynamics, which birthed the concept, it is very specifically defined as the Second Law of Thermodynamics. Britannica defines, "The measure of a system's thermal energy per unit temperature that is unavailable for doing useful work."

Without going into a long discourse trying to define entropy, thermodynamically, if you place two objects of different temperatures together, they will eventually equalize to the same temperature. Heat from the hotter object will transfer to the cooler object. In this sense, the hotter object is more ordered, the cooler less. Generalized, entropy is the movement of a more ordered system to being less ordered. Importantly, it doesn't work in reverse. The less order, the greater entropy.

In the 19th century, physicist James Clerk Maxwell developed a thought experiment where it was possible to develop an anti-entropy process. The idea was controlling a door in the middle of a box of equally dispersed moving particles of various velocities. Maxwell called this process a demon. By continually opening the door with specific timing, the demon could gradually gather on one side of the box all the fastest moving particles, raising the temperature on that side of the box, thus violating the Second Law and reducing entropy.

A half-century later, Hungarian physicist Leo Szilard wrote a paper entitled, "On the reduction of entropy in a thermodynamic system by the intervention of an intelligent being." Szilard figured out Maxwell's demon was really introducing information into the system. Applied information can reduce entropy, creating greater order. Some would argue, this is in a sense a definition of life. Across its existence all life creates new order by reordering energy.

The concept of entropy is fundamental to Claude Shannon's Information Theory, basically figuring out what amounts of data are necessary for a message to be orderly transferred, that is communicated not just as jumbled data, but understandable information. With our present information technologies, this is accomplished by the information equivalent of brute force, all requiring ever vaster amounts of energy.

Our present information technologies are a massive energy sink. Scharf writes, "Our computational data centers alone are already using an amount of energy comparable to the entire planet's output in the early 1800s."

He adds alarmingly, "A study in 2016 by the Semiconductor Industry Association in the US produced a road map assessment of where things looked to be headed. The bleak prediction: by sometime around 2040 the world's computer chips will demand more electricity than is expected to be produced globally."

This is both unsustainable development and an unobtainable end.

However, it makes very clear why in an era of tightening and more expensive fossil fuel supplies combined with the increasing impact of humanity's past and present energy use on the greater planetary ecology, the Tech industry is a great nuclear power advocate. Nukes have plenty of problems, but with current energy usage growth rates, those of information technologies alone would be impossible to meet with any feasible addition of nuclear generation.

Nor will we be capable of just plugging into various renewable generation sources to meet such future demand. As Scharf writes, "The issue is not that we necessarily run out of electricity, but that infrastructure for generating ever more power consumes ever more resources (in rare earths or lithium for batteries and their manufacture, copper cabling, or sheer land area)." The land area issue is a fossil fuel industry induced red herring. Renewables can be sourced across already human inhabited areas and integrated in such a way to be relatively unintrusive, but that still leaves the very important resource questions.

Years ago, working on energy issues, I was talking with a friend and colleague, a physicist, Rich Ferguson. I was always and remain a great solar advocate, but I said something flippant. Rich looked at me, smiled, and said, "There's no such thing as free energy." This is true both locally and universally. There is the ability and necessity to change our present energy sources, design more efficient energy systems, and to be much more energy wise. This is very difficult to do when there's entrenched power, and entrenched economic and social habits reliant on present usage. This includes exorbitant energy waste and maybe most difficult to change, the idea this waste is wealth.

In this regard, information technologies create vast amounts of information and energy waste. Scharf writes, "Every idea is a burden in some way or other, whether in biological metabolism or technological energy demands, but not every idea is equal in its value or utility." This might be the most invaluable insight of the book.

Spending any time on the internet, you're instantly deluged by vast amounts of information waste, seeking to sell more waste. The production, communication, and intellectual processing of this information all need time and energy. We presently value information in context of the industrial values of more – more energy, more resources, more stuff, no matter what it is, more is better. Quantitative value quashes qualitative. A revaluation of industrial values is required. Cutting information waste reduces energy waste. But also flipping this, we can use information to cut energy waste. Our entrenched industrial infrastructure and processes can be redesigned to be more energy and resource efficient.

Our current energy technologies operate entirely on quantitative value. One different understanding, and there needs to be many, to our present information technologies energy waste lies in a better understanding of ourselves and the ecological systems from which we evolved. For instance, Scharf points out, "Biological brains are approximately a billion times *more efficient* than current standard microprocessor capabilities." Biological brain functions are not binary, though it's fashionable to try and understand and model as such, and no doubt some specific knowledge can be gained in doing so.

However, Scharf writes, "Humans themselves are multicellular things, composed of perhaps 30 trillion or more cells in total, together with at least as many single-celled microbial passengers." These systems are not binary or run by algorithms. They are not centrally controlled. We are amazingly complex, incredibly distributed systems. There is no CEO cell or President microbe anywhere in our bodies. There is great energy value to this decentralized information and communication architecture, value we little understand or appreciate. In developing future information systems and networks, indeed all physical infrastructure, and social and political organization, we need to explore the workings and design of distributed network architectures.

It is increasingly clear this specialized way of treating information, defined by physics, this narrow perspective, must change with the addition of more inclusive, complex perspectives, particularly regarding information's and energy's interaction in regards to biological organisms and their relation with the greater ecological systems from which they evolved. Just as Bohr's complementarity showed with an understanding of classical and quantum physics, the latter doesn't overthrow the former, both become necessary for complete understanding, so too a more complex understanding of information is necessary.

This is where Scharf's book falls most short, doing so because he and many he chronicles want to create a unified information theory. Unfortunately, the more he attempts to introduce a unified general definition, the less informative the book, especially due to the analogies and metaphors he uses. He unhelpfully employs a long list of ideas we understand specifically or in many cases misunderstand, such as "viruses cheat," "genes choose," and "life is an algorithm." Most distressing, the idea the world is one big computer and *"Life on Earth is nothing more than a four-billion-year-old catalytic chemical computation."* (his italics)

Analogy and metaphors are essential in helping explain many ideas in science. It is using the known to help conceptualize something previously unknown. When science comes up with truly new concepts, they are the most difficult to convey. What we already know limits our initial understanding to anything truly new. History is full of new technologies being used to define the universe – clocks, steam engines, and now most unfortunately computers.

It's inadvisable to attempt devising a general information theory, but especially by taking very specific scientific understandings and their technological progeny and trying to generalize them as laws of the universe. More important and a great deal more valuable is understanding all technology has developed in very specific contexts, their very being excluding wider, existentially necessary perspectives. At this point, doubling down on only what we know and what has already been engineered isn't going to do anybody any good.

ARENDT, INFORMATION, & DEMOCRACY

I recently ran across a great interview with Hannah Arendt from 1964. Amazing how relevant her remarks remain, when most of what is said today is worthless tomorrow. In one part of the interview, she gets to the nut of politics, which is who makes the decisions and how that process is structured and organized, essentially including what information is used in determining any decision.

Arendt talks about how perspective plays a great role in how we process information. Speaking at the end of the Modern Era, she notes individual perspective is increasingly confused, an individual's orientation in the larger society problematic. She says,

"First of all, this inability to be truly oriented applies not only to the general populace, but every other stratum of society, I would even say to the statesman."

"The statesman is surrounded, encircled by an army of experts. And actually, the question of action here is between the statesman and the experts. The statesman has to make the final decision. He can hardly do that realistically, since he can't know everything himself. He has to take from experts, from experts who in principle always must contradict each other."

This is a fundamental understanding of the structure of information processing that grew across modern society. Even those at the top, and where Arendt is using statesman, you could just as well substitute CEO, "can't know everything." The statesman is responsible for bringing about the separate specialists' (experts) understandings into a generalized whole, in so doing deciding the public. Through the statesman, this combination of specialist understanding and decision making is politics.

She continues,

"Every reasonable statesman gets opposing expert opinions because he has to see the issue from all sides. He has to judge between them and this judging is an extremely mysterious process in which the community spirit is to be expressed."

This is an especially important point. In the past, any effective statesman would seek a variety of advice. Today, that's not so true, established thinking seeks only reinforcement. In addition, in the political realm, established views come attached to established power, who have zero interest in seeking a wider spectrum of views and the power to drastically narrow the spectrum. It is not by accident one seeks in vain any public figure today who could rise to the once respected title of statesman — no matter what gender.

Next, Arendt talks about the same process of information availability and decision making among the general public:

> "Now, as far as the populace is concerned, I would say wherever people come together, it doesn't matter the size, public interests come into play and the public sphere is formed. And in America, where there are still these spontaneous associations, which then split up again, the kind of associations that Tocqueville already described, you can see this very clearly."

> "Some public interests concern a specific group of people, in a neighborhood, or even a house, or in a city, or some other sort of group. Then these people will get together and be very good at being able to act publicly in these matters since they oversee them."

> "And there, believe me, the difference between the statesman and the man on the street in principle isn't very great."

This is an excellent democratic understanding. When Arendt was speaking, the associations first documented by Tocqueville as fundamental to democracy in America, still existed, though greatly deteriorated. Today, they barely exist, thus, so too, democracy in America. These associations were organized information processes, people came together defining and creating public. Democratically organized, these associations pluralistically decided as opposed to the individual statesman's decree.

Arendt lays out the politics of information, which in this century has become an even more essential component of society. Our current societal organization of information is entirely specialized. Little value is placed in bringing together disparate specializations to create the whole — the public. It is the failure of politics.

Today, specialization creates an infinity of experts, who are incessantly trotted out as advocates or rationalizers for any given action, representing the limited expertise of established interests. Alternatives are shunted aside with decision making becoming ever more centralized.

In regards to the inability of any person in this era to know everything or even know any one thing, the key questions are what information is used to make decisions and who makes decisions. In a society ruled by specialist expertise, the wise words from another era of Justice Louis Brandeis prove useful:

> "My early associations were such as to give me greater reverence than I now have for the things that are because they are. I recall that when I began to practice law I thought it awkward, stupid, and vulgar that a jury of twelve inexpert men should have the power to decide. I had the greatest respect for the judge. I trusted only expert opinion. Experience of life has made me democratic. I began to see that many things sanctioned by expert opinion and denounced by popular opinion were wrong."

In decision making processes, we can all be equal. How public decisions are made defines politics. A democratic reform of politics begins with reorganizing the current architecture of information, a necessary explosion of associations providing perspective, networked together to create new public space.

In this regard, Arendt concludes,

> "Politics is action, all action is a venture, this venture is only possible with trust in humanity, which means, quite difficult to precisely formulate, but a fundamental trust in what's human in all people. Otherwise it couldn't exist."

I've long asserted belief in mythical gods is easy, faith in your very real fellow human beings, very difficult, it's tested every god damn day.

MONEY REFORM AND INFORMATION

I recently received an email from a friend that included this money chart created by a financial firm called TrendCompass:

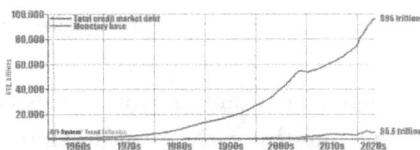

Using Fed numbers, this is just a great graphic charting the last decades financialization of the economy. The top black line is "credit," aka debt, while the bottom line is the "monetary base" or cash money. I don't want to get into the semantics of money, oh lord that's funny, talk to the Fed if you got problems, but what the chart shows is the financial system leveraged 20 times. Over the course of its acceptance, through trial and era, it became a sort of a rule of thumb that 10 to 1 leverage promoted financial stability in the modern bank-debt money system and so, well, here we are.

The numbers don't include derivatives, which according to the Bank of International Settlements in 2022 amounted to $634 trillion globally. That's six times more than the total debt. Most derivatives are just an accounting scam, fraud some might say, on various entities' books, most cancel each other out. However, the BIS notes, "The gross market value of outstanding OTC derivatives, summing positive and negative values, rose noticeably in the first half of 2022, to $18.3 trillion, led by increases in interest rate derivatives." That's a lot of cash money someone would need to pony up if the money system started shaking like it did in 2008.

Remember, always a funny term when talking to Americans, the Financial Crisis Inquiry Commission's 2011 report stated unregulated derivatives were "a key turning point in the march toward the financial crisis." I'm on record way back then, the day report was released, saying it would never be talked about again. But, here you go Byron, once again you can say, "Costello wrong again. How that guy even types a keystroke is simply ridiculousness."

The explosion in derivatives was the last gift Mr. Bill bequeathed to the monied class right before he left office signing the "Commodity Futures Modernization Act." That codified such wonderful things as, "No provision of the Commodity Exchange Act shall apply to, and the Commodity Futures Trading Commission shall not regulate, a hybrid instrument (derivative)," and better, "This title shall supersede and preempt the application of any State or local law that prohibits or regulates gaming or the operation of bucket shops" – Oh Bubba! Who knew in his '92 Democratic acceptance speech when Mr. Bill rhapsodized about a "New Covenant," he was actually talking about a new felonious bank covenant?

Well, enough bad nostalgia. As far as the stability of the financial system, place your bets. Money is and has always been a work in progress. But such numbers do reveal several things. First, while the modern bank-debt money system was never democratic (see the Populists), it is far more undemocratic than ever, an entrenched money oligarchy with a great interest in sustaining an unsustainable status quo, the only way the debt can be repaid.

Secondly and more importantly, as an information medium in a self-proclaimed market system, money has become increasingly valueless in regards to its information content. Technology historian Marshall McLuhan wrote in *Understanding Media*,

> "Money, had been for many centuries the principal transmitter and exchanger of information... Money is a language for translating the work of the farmer into the work of the barber, doctor, engineer, or plumber. As a vast social metaphor, bridge, or translator, money – like writing – speeds up exchange and tightens the bonds of interdependence in any community."

The information content of money was and is always critically dependent on the greater information environment of the society as a whole. McLuhan writes,

> "Shortly before the advent of paper money, the greatly increased volume of information movement in European newsletters and newspapers created the image and concept of National Credit. Such a corporate image of credit depended, then as now, on the fast and comprehensive information movement that we have taken for granted for two centuries and more."

Like all information, the information value of money is dependent on its communication, and as McLuhan notes, paper currency, to the consternation of every gold bug, facilitated and necessitated much faster communication,

> "Representative money, based on print technology, created new speedy dimensions of credit that were quite inconsistent with the inert mass of bullion and of commodity money. Yet all efforts were bent to make the speedy new money behave like the slow bullion coach."

Until the creation of the Fed in 1913, money was still largely based on metals, but this changed over the next six decades, money was completely relieved of its gold weights.

The growth of debt since 1980 directly correlates with the growth of the computer industry and electronic money. With computers came an exponential rise in information, information moving at the speed of light, along with the necessity of this information being monetarily valued for utilization. Yet, modern society's predominate or even exclusive valuing of all information monetarily degenerated the value of money, simultaneously distorting and diminishing the value of information.

McLuhan writes, "Apart from communal participation, money is meaningless." Money has always been and always will be a political medium. Information and communication have always been fundamental elements of politics, of all human social organization. Now, information is fundamental in reshaping the greater physical environment surrounding us. Looking from this perspective, we see the political system itself has become ever more flooded with money and thus increasingly dysfunctional. The corporation, one way or other the source of most political money, is itself a creation of money. Incapable of anything except monetary valuation, the ability of the corporation itself to effectively utilize the ever vaster flood of information also falters.

Such a situation cries not just for reforming money, as the crypto-crowd so poorly advocates, but the reform of politics, government and all our associations, including corporations, enabling them to value information without having to exclusively transform it into monetary value. It's very difficult in an era now completely dominated by money for us to understand or even conceive of non-monetary value, especially true when an oligarchy of money demands subservience. Yet, across human history most information was created, communicated, and valued non-monetarily. For example, our dilapidated democracy still has the remnants of the vote, a non-monetary value system, though now completely dominated by money.

While money, one way or other, has always had information content, the monetary value of all information is new. In the last four decades, enormous amounts of debt have been created, in part, as an attempt to value the exponential explosion of information. It is a losing game for the value of both money and information.

THE POLITICS OF SCIENCE

WHERE DO WE COME FROM? WHAT ARE WE? WHERE ARE WE GOING?

History is the medium of politics. Without knowledge of history, politics becomes untethered, suspect, of little worth. History will never be a science as it cannot be reset and repeated to prove any given theory. It's impenetrable to the scientific method, the very process that created modernity, yet history remains essential for answering, as Gauguin asked, "Where do we come from? What are we? Where are we going?" More invaluable than ever, history is lost today, deflated to worthlessness by jaundiced focus and buried by technology, science's omnipotent societal shaping force.

Last century birthed great insights in historical studies, maybe none greater than Fernand Braudel's, *The Mediterranean and the Mediterranean World in the Age of Philip II,* a seminal work rewriting historical understanding. In the introduction Braudel sets out his wonderful theory of history, comparing it to numerous intersecting currents of various depths and speeds. Deep at the bottom, moving slowly, largely beyond the constructs of an average human life, even beyond the perception of ages, are the shaping forces of geography, geology, and climate. Bodies of waters such as the Mediterranean, its surrounding mountain ranges, vast plains, and deserts, change little over the course of millennia, fundamentally shaping each society built around and across them.

Braudel writes,

"(It is) history that is almost changeless, the history of man in relation to his surroundings. It is history which unfolds slowly and is slow to alter, often repeating itself and working itself out in cycles which are endlessly renewed... which exists almost out of time and tells the story of man's contact with the inanimate."

Easy examples are Egypt's five-thousand year history shaped today as it was five-thousand years ago by vast desert and the narrow ribbon of lush life produced by the Nile flowing from the far away mountains of inner Africa. Or Istanbul, across thousands of years, whether Greek, Roman, Christian or Muslim, shaped by its position on the Bosphorus Strait connecting the Black Sea to the north and the Mediterranean to the south.

Above and through these deeper currents flow the histories of societies, the "history of gentle rhythms, of groups and groupings...economies and states, societies and civilizations." These currents are not as deep or fundamental as geography, they move faster, maybe a little, though not necessarily better, understood by the peoples whose lives they direct.

History's surface currents Braudel refers to as *l'historie evenementielle*, the movement of contemporary events by individuals, "a surface disturbance, the waves stirred up by the powerful movement of tides." Braudel warns these events, emotionally charged for the participants and those who immediately follow, in many ways offer the least historical knowledge. Poetically writing of the seduction of contemporary events, Braudel states,

"We must beware of that history which still simmers with the passions of the contemporaries who felt it, described it, lived it, to the rhythm of their brief lives, lives as brief as are our own...

A world of vivid passions certainly, but a blind world, as any living world must be, as ours is, oblivious of the deep currents of history, of those living waters on which our frail barks are tossed..."

Adding,

"A perilous world, granted, but one whose spells and dangerous enchantments we will have exorcised by having previously charted those great underlying currents which so often run silently, and whose true significance emerges only if one can observe their workings over great spans of time. Resounding events often take place in an instant, and are but manifestations of that larger destiny by which alone they can be explained."

Nonetheless, through this current of superficial events our short lives interact with history. For any given time, the determinant of health for any politics depends on how well history is incorporated into its movements and decisions. Unknowingly, the Modern Era experienced powerful movements of the deeper and slower currents of history catalyzing the more ephemeral surface events. Paradoxically, the rise of these deep currents were the result of historically unprecedented technological development. The complete lack in understanding of these historical movements and the seeming ahistorical identity of technology leaves contemporary civilization without politics, moved violently by events we neither direct or understand.

In better understanding the present era, *The Age of Phillip II* offers an excellent perspective, a truly remarkable Mediterranean era that saw the peak of the Renaissance, the opening of the Americas to Europe, Spain's affluence, significant cultural change, a flourishing of intellect in the cities, and on its eastern shore the rise of the Ottomans, Islam's last great empire.

The Age of Phillip II is an excellent example of history's various currents moving, crossing, resurfacing and submerging. Encouraged by the fall of Constantinople in 1452, the thought of ancient Greece and Rome resurfaced across Italy and eventually much of Europe. Islam's triumph saw the end of the last vestiges of the Roman empire, while the rise of Ottomans was the culmination of the Turks long migration out of northeast Mongolia beginning thousands of years before. Constantinople's Christian refugees clutched what they could of their libraries and using the new printing press helped reintroduce ancient Greek and Roman pagan thought to the "West."

This world, still shaped by the ancient Mediterranean itself, produced the actions of the Medici, Borgia, Michelangelo, da Vinci, Montaigne, Machiavelli, Suleiman the Magnificent, Phillip II, and endless others. Even with all this, Braudel emphasizes history's deep currents,

"The Mediterranean in the sixteenth century was overwhelmingly a world of peasants, of tenant farmers and anything else was superstructure, the result of accumulation and of unnatural diversion towards the towns. Peasants and crops, in other words food supplies and size of population, silently determined the destiny of the age. In both the long and the short term, agricultural life was all-important. Could it support the burden of increasing population and luxury of an urban civilization so dazzling that it has blinded us to other things? For each succeeding generation this was the pressing problem of every day. Beside it, the rest seems to dwindle into insignificance."

The era's most important name for the future was Galileo, who helped start a most radical and new culture. Galileo represents the beginning of modern science that would develop into the most powerful historical force of the past several centuries. Indeed, the Industrial Era's stark demarcation from the entire ten-thousand year Agrarian Era preceding it was the mass movement of people out of the fields and into towns and cities. Using the US as grossest example, the republic's founding saw close to 90% of the population involved in agriculture, a century later just over half. Today, less than 2% of the American population is directly involved in agriculture. Globally, it is estimated only one billion of the earth's present eight billion people are farmers — 13%.

Science instigated this great migration. With Galileo's laws of motion, humanity began understanding the physics of mass and force. Over the next two-centuries, ever more rapidly growing scientific understanding led to the innovation of industrial technologies powered by our abilities to harness the power of energy from burning fossil fuels. This scientific revolution developed from a deep current of history, the long evolution of *Homo Sapiens'* abstract intellect, which began at least as far back as our Homo ancestors, two or three million years ago. Over the last two centuries, this ability for abstract thought exploded our knowledge, but by no means wisdom, of nature at its deepest and most fundamental levels.

The most forceful technological currents of the last two centuries flowed from the burning of fossil fuels. Intriguingly, fossil fuels would be firmly entrenched in Braudel's deepest, slowest moving, barely perceptible historical currents – geology. The surfacing of these currents shaped *Homo sapiens* life at an unprecedentedly rapid rate to an unparalleled degree. The formation of fossil fuels (coal, oil, natural gas) occurred several hundred million years ago, slowly fermenting over millions of years with pressures from rock pressing down and heat rising from the planet's core. Fossil fuels are the remnants of ancient life, storing the energy of ancient sunlight. Coal was largely formed from the great forests and swamps of the last period of the Paleozoic Era. Oil followed in the Mesozoic Era from great blankets of algae and zooplankton covering the earth's vast seas.

Designed by our several million year old intellect, the burning of fossil fuels from the earth's ancient past literally transformed the entire planet's landscape and atmosphere. Braudel's deep, slow moving past was rapidly brought forth into contemporary time, radically altering how we interact with our surroundings, previously history's slower, deeper, and dominant shaping forces.

All technology homogenizes. Diversity is replaced by a sameness created by any given technology's influence. Maybe fossil fuels greatest homogenizing impact has been on plant and animal life, replacing once great roaming hordes and diversity of animals with a relatively few corralled and caged species. While once an innumerable variety of plants, human edible plants particularly, were dramatically narrowed to a handful such as corn, rice, and wheat.

In regards to climate, heating and cooling systems can make a frozen landscape temperate, a tropical environment cool. Fossil fuel transportation shrinks, levels, and transcends geographical boundaries, eliminating mountain barriers and shrinking the once vast separation of oceans. Most recently, we've discovered reintroducing massive amounts of ancient organic carbon without a corresponding revitalizing of life leaves seas of carbon in the atmosphere, changing centuries and even millennia old weather patterns

It's also essential to understand the laws of physics from which industrial technologies were created are much more ancient than fossil fuels. Older than the planet itself, they are the fundamental laws of the universe. The last century witnessed even more radical technologies developed with even more fundamental quantum physics. This understanding instantaneously birthed new unprecedentedly powerful technologies, including nuclear weaponry and the transistor. These technologies, based on the most ancient and fundamental workings of the universe, can conceivably alter all established geographic boundaries, culture, and human practices, in ways redefining what it is to be human.

In utilizing this recent knowledge, *Homo sapiens* transcend history to a greater degree than with industrialization. However, the perceived novelty of quantum technology in reality remains very much as anciently defined as the first stone tool. As Braudel stated the deep currents of history, almost imperceptible to an average life, concern humanity's contact with the inanimate. These new technologies are in a real sense the animation of the inanimate, creating overwhelming societal forces. Quantum physics delves into the eternal dance of the universe's basic order of mass and energy.

Since the dawn of industrialization, even much more in the last decades, it is tempting to forget and disregard history. Yet, history remains our only and quite insufficient measure of technology's value. Without history, the determinative value of technological development becomes technology itself, a most unnatural, indeed a completely asocial selection system. Technological evolution neither constrained or uninfluenced by any larger environment is a process not simply ahistorical, but in relation to the evolution of life, completely unnatural.

The last century also saw an explosive growth in human understanding of the history of life on earth. Paleontology, anthropology and evolutionary biology further opened the deep past of *Homo Sapiens* and far beyond. Using this knowledge, particularly with biology, we rapidly move to develop technologies, again, with little understanding of life's long history, overwhelming the very deep historical forces of natural selection. Biological evolution can only be understood as an historical process.

Most ironically, recent decades have seen the rise of a new, spurious theology, based not on any metaphysical faith in the past, but unwarranted worship of technology itself. Humanity's long past search for metaphysical meaning in nature, ancient scrolls and the preaching of prophets is replaced by a ridiculous faith in technology's unknowable future. Evangelized across the Industrial Age with the nebulous term of progress, today's technological faith is preached by priesthoods of technologists with the mantra, "It cannot be stopped." Humanity is becoming locked into an unending, ever quickening, ever changing race with no finish line — a blind faith, not in ourselves, but in technology. It is an ahistorical mindset and ignorance of terrifying proportions.

One only need look at the still unaccounted changes brought about by industrialism, most especially in regards to its impact on innumerable ecological systems and the greater global environment, to understand this faith is not simply misplaced, but exceedingly childish, the wisdom of a toddler barreling down a hallway grasping a razor sharp butcher's knife.

Our technological evolution necessitates a greatly broadened sense of history, an even more essential understanding. Braudel's beautiful and valuable look at history as a series of intersecting currents of variable strengths, speeds, and depths had one fault, it didn't go back nearly far enough. In many ways a traditional historian, Braudel did not include older understandings of "prehistoric" *Homo sapiens* or biological and physical science. Since his death, just our historical understanding of the genus Homo, expanding back millions of years, has grown exponentially. Prehistorical understandings essential to knowing where we as a species came from, how we were shaped, and who we still very much remain in the 21st century. Deeper historical understanding is essential to both dealing with the still unaddressed legacies of industrialism and to in any way healthily utilize an entirely new generation of rapidly developing information and biological technologies. Absent history, we have no compass, no direction, the future is all *terra incognita,* and we are tossed by the waves without even a ship.

POLITICAL SCIENCE

Science is inherently political. This is not meant in any way to degrade science, but reveals a most desperate need to reform politics by incorporating science into politics, while simultaneously developing an understanding of the politics of science. The other day some of our Tech Priests were evangelizing a "God-AI." Lord, which fucking one? If it's Quetzalcoatl God-AI, these United States got an ass-whooping coming, something to think about my fellow Americans.

A half-century ago, one of history's greatest thinkers on democracy, Hannah Arendt, astutely defined our present predicament. Arendt thought about how to reform the latest iteration of democracy – modern republicanism. One thing she emphasized is all democracy at its core is about taking action, an understanding in direct opposition to much anti-democratic propaganda by its modern detractors. Arendt rightly perceived action as the goal of all politics. If it is to be democracy, every citizen is part of both deciding the action to take and helping in its implementation.

Arendt explained innate to this idea is with any action there is a beginning. This beginning is a fundamental political freedom. She writes,

> "Perhaps the best illustration within the arena of Greek politics that freedom of action is the same thing as starting anew and beginning something is the word *archein* means both to begin and to lead. The twofold meaning manifestly indicates that originally the term 'leader' was used for the person who initiated something and sought out companions to help him carry it

out; and this carrying out, this bringing something that has been begun to its end, was the original meaning for the word action, *prattein*. The same linkage between being free and beginning something is found in the Roman idea that the greatness of the forebears was contained in the founding of Rome, and that the freedom of the Romans always had to be traced to this founding—*ab urbe condita*—where a beginning had been made."

The American republic long and rightly celebrated its founding generation. With all their faults they began, they acted, they were free. However, after two centuries, their founding institutions increasingly became not facilitators of action, of new beginnings, but a straight jacket limiting both citizen decision making and action. Writing in mid-20th century New York, Arendt critiqued the state of modern republicanism, participatory decision making, all resulting citizen action largely illusory. Limited in a number of ways from the beginning, at that point American democracy existed not much at all.

With industrial society, Arendt astutely points out American politics, the political ability to begin and act, had largely become the exclusive enfranchisement of scientists and technologists. She writes,

"The capacity for action, at least in the sense of the releasing of processes, is still with us, although it has become the exclusive prerogative of the scientists, who have enlarged the realm of human affairs to the point of extinguishing the time honored protective dividing line between nature and the human world. In view of such achievements, performed for centuries in the unseen quiet of the laboratories, it seems only proper that their deeds should eventually have turned out to have greater news value, to be of greater political significance, than the administrative and diplomatic doings of most so-called statesmen. It certainly is not without irony that those whom public opinion has persistently held to be the least practical and the least political members of society should have turned out to be the only ones left who still know how to act and how to act in concert. For their early organizations, which they founded in the seventeenth century for the conquest of nature and in which they developed their own moral standards and their own code of honor, have not only survived all vicissitudes of the modern age, but they have become one of the most potent power-generating groups in all history."

One of the first and foremost of these organizations, far and away becoming the most politically dominant force in industrial life, is the corporation. The corporation has never been democratically organized, at best it's an oligarchy. It is the corporation with ever new technology and a significant amount of government organizational support, that has most powerfully attempted to conquer nature. And there's the rub.

Through science we learn how nature operates. Science can be a most sublime and quite beautiful process. Science tells us what has been, how things have come to be operate. However, science does not necessarily tell us the future, despite the hopes and dreams of more than a few scientists who believe all they need to be prophets is the right amount of data. Two foundational sciences, quantum physics and biological evolution, measure uncertainty at the bottom of all action and life as in part random mutation, selected not by the deeds of the individual, but the ever changing forces designing each species.

Science facilitates our inventions of technology based on the workings of nature. Science does not tell us in what ways we should develop any technology, that is in what fashion, and most importantly, whether we should even develop any given technology.

Historically, all democratic institutions – Athens, Rome, and the US – have been of the Agrarian Era, largely pre-science and pre-industrial. At best, America's republican institutions have been grandly insufficient dealing with modernity's literally universal increase in scientific knowledge and the resulting technological offspring. Arendt writes,

"The modern astrophysical world view, which began with Galileo, and its challenge to the adequacy of the senses to reveal reality, have left us a universe of whose qualities we know no more than the way they affect our measuring instruments, and —in the words of Eddington—'the former have as much resemblance to the latter as a telephone number has to a subscriber.' Instead of objective qualities, in other words, we find instruments, and instead of nature or the universe—in the words of Heisenberg—man encounters only himself."

Arthur Eddington was the astronomer who confirmed Einstein's Relativity, the understanding to the great discomfort of many of the inherently subjective measurement of the universe's most fundamental forces. While Werner Heisenberg was most influential in developing quantum physics. Who knew just a few years later Heisenberg would prove to be a good German? Well, he wasn't the only one. As an educated German of his era, Heisenberg could not only do math, but had a great Classical education. He would be familiar with Aristotle's fundamental insight, "By nature, man is a political animal." And if Heisenberg is right that through science we find in nature only ourselves, science is politics.

ENTANGLED LIFE

In many ways, biology is the newest science. Not that in the Western tradition, some aspects of biological thought haven't been around since the Greeks. After all, Aristotle had a great deal to say on the designs of life. But the history of life, the knowledge no organism stands alone, that a species is only defined in relation to its greater environment, have only been fitfully understood for not much more than a century. Ecology, an essential biological concept, was only developed by the German naturalist Ernst Haeckel at the end of the 19th century.

In the last couple decades, good biology books started to appear more frequently. At the very top of this list is 2020's *Entangled Life,* by Merlin Sheldrake, an amazingly thought provoking look at fungi, a life form still little studied or understood, yet all knowledge we gain challenges our established thinking on life, its organization, connections, and functions. Understanding fungi offers us a greater understanding of ecology,

"The study of the relationships between organisms and their environments: both the places where they live and the thicket of relationships that sustain them. Inspired by the work of Alexander von Humboldt, the study of ecology emerged from the idea that nature is an interconnected whole, 'a system of active forces.' Organisms could not be understood in isolation."

Everyone has experienced a fungus. Beer and bread come from our cultivation of yeast fungi. We may have also experienced various fungi causing bodily infections or plant debilitation. Everyone's encountered molds and mildews. Mushrooms and truffles are fungal fruit, considered dietary staples and delicacies across the planet. Fungi range in size from single celled yeast to honey fungi, among the largest organisms on the planet. In Oregon, one honey fungus specimen weighs eight hundred tons, spread across six square miles. It is thought to be somewhere between two to eight thousand years old!

In traditional and maybe increasingly archaic biological taxonomy, fungi are their own kingdom, alongside bacteria, plants, and animals. At a foundational organizational level and quite contradictory from appearance, fungi are closer to animals than plants. In the history of life, fungi developed before both plants and animals. It is thought photosynthesizing algae, first moving to land 600 million years ago, partnered with fungi to get necessary minerals and water from the soil, out of this relationship evolved plants. There's believed to be two to three million fungal species living both on land and sea, more fungi species than plants and animals combined.

Entangled Life is marvelously thought provoking. The more we understand about fungi, the more a great deal of our established thought about how life operates is challenged and upended. I'll break down some of the book's ideas into two, though adopting some fungal understanding, by no means exclusive parts.

First, this piece looks at fungal interactions with their environment and the radical reshaping of established biological thought this entails. Second, a look at the structural organization and processes of the fungal organisms themselves, provoking thought on how *Homo sapiens* organize both socially and in relation to our greater environment.

The most revolutionary change induced by understanding fungi is the concept of symbiosis, developed by 19th century German botanist Albert Frank's study of lichens. Anyone who has traveled across mountains, through deserts, or walked past old stone walls is familiar with lichen, the brilliant, multicolored geometric patterns covering rocks. When first encountered, it's difficult to believe lichens are a life form. Yet, they are essential actors in breaking down those very mountains, boulders, and rocks into the soil necessary for plants to grow.

Lichens are fungi, but more importantly, they are fungi partnering with algae and bacteria. By destructing the rocks, fungi provide the minerals and water for the photosynthetic algae and or bacteria, which in return provide sun produced energy in the form of sugars to the fungi. Frank created the term symbiosis to describe this partnership.

"The biologist Heinrich Anton de Bary adopted Frank's term and generalized it to refer to the full type of interactions between any type of organism, stretching from parasitism at one pole, to mutually beneficial relationships at the other."

Sheldrake writes,

"Lichens were a gateway organism to the idea of symbiosis, an idea that ran against the prevailing currents in evolutionary thought in the late-nineteenth century and early twentieth centuries, best summed up in Thomas Henry Huxley's portrayal of life as a 'gladiator's show...whereby the strongest, the swiftest, and the cunningest live to fight another day.' In the wake of the dual hypothesis, evolution could no longer be thought of solely in terms of competition and conflict. Lichens had become a type case of inter-kingdom collaboration."

Symbiosis runs counter to evolutionary thinking of not just a century ago, but still most established thinking on evolution today. Symbiosis has yet to be greatly incorporated into evolutionary thinking. Not that the idea of symbiosis is in anyway inconsistent with Darwin's essential insight, which was not about the individual's struggle for existence. Darwin's "natural selection" is about species', not individual's design being determined by its greater environment. Symbiosis is a process of natural selection.

Even more radical to our present thinking is the organizational structure and internal processes of the fungi themselves. The great fungal networks—mycelia, are examples of distributed, decentralized order, demanding a needed reassessment of our hierarchical, centralized thinking, including a healthy expansion of our ideas on intelligence. As Sheldrake writes, by looking at the structure of fungi, "Some of the vexed hierarchies that underpin modern thought start to soften."

While many fungi-like yeasts are single cell,

"Most fungi form networks of many cells known as hyphae: fine tubular structures that branch, fuse, and tangle into the anarchic filigree of mycelium. Mycelium describes the most common of fungal habits, better thought of not as a thing but a process: an exploratory, irregular tendency. Water and nutrients flow through ecosystems within mycelial networks."

Looking at the mycelium, the fungal network (shown above), it's important to notice there is no center. They are distributedly ordered. We know little about the functioning of true distributed networks, including, as Sheldrake makes clear, fungi.

Most of the action is at the tip, known as the hyphal.

"Hyphal tips are the parts of the mycelium that grow, change direction, branch, and fuse. They are the part of the mycelium that do the most. And they are numerous. A given mycelial network might have anywhere between hundreds and billions of hyphal tips, all integrating and processing information on a massively parallel basis."

"Mycelial coordination is difficult to understand because there is no center of control. Fungi, like plants, are decentralized organisms. There are no operational centers, no capital cities, no seats of government. Control is dispersed: Mycelial coordination takes place both everywhere at a once and nowhere in particular. A fragment of mycelium can regenerate an entire network."

All of this is completely radical to our notions of organization and processes. With fungi, there is no hierarchy of control as we now "believe" in animals. Knowledge about fungi will give us a better understanding of how we actually function opposed to the many stories we fabricate and tell ourselves.

HEISENBERG AGONISTES: PROGRESS

Long ago, I quit reading philosophy – credit or blame Nietzsche. Immediately after, I read a number of the 20th century physicists who were immensely educational and enjoyable. In ways, it was philosophy of a different sort. Many of the best had extensive knowledge of the Greeks, the intellectual roots, all agreed, fundamental to physics itself. Recently, I reread a few of these essential thinkers, instigated by the recent popular promotion/shilling of Artificial Intelligence (AI), the latest generation of computer technology, a technology itself developed with knowledge gained from 20th century physics.

The preceding generation of computing was defined by the networking of computers, most especially the internet. I became aware of the internet three decades ago, just as home and business desktop computers started to connect. Simultaneously, I had removed myself from the campaign election game, which continued spiraling down as quickly as the internet exploded up. However, my interest in politics, in the largest sense, didn't diminish. Most of the physicists I read, including Einstein, Bohr, Heisenberg, and Oppenheimer, all helped bring about the Quantum Era, insisted a healthy politics was not only necessary, but more essential than ever.

In the 90s, I spent a lot of time thinking about, though entirely incapable of acting on the idea the internet could prove useful for (in fact its very implementation demanded) an American political renaissance, particularly, a reformation of democracy. Yet this turned out to be impossible for two important reasons. First, the increasingly debauched decline of traditional politics in America, and secondly, the culture of creating instant vast tech fortunes as the overwhelming measure of value in weighing the worth of any given technology. Americans' love of technology is only surpassed by veneration for those who pile up quick fortunes: the greater the pile, the greater the adoration. Three decades later, our politics are even more dysfunctional, wealth as the determinant in decision making entirely unchecked and unbalanced.

So, in regards to AI, it's unsurprising to see our self-professed, self-deluding, apolitical tech oligarchy repeating the same nonpolitical arguments of the early 90s, such as "tech development can't be stopped." Hell, it seemingly can't even be influenced. What's especially alarming, more accurately quite depressing, is the development of this next generation of compute technology is largely being led by the fortunes created by the internet, the last couple decades of "social media" wealth. You'd be hard pressed to prove the world is in anyway a better place because of Facebook, Twitter, Linkedin et al., but money was made, big money.

Unsurprisingly, the FT ran a piece by a pudgy, soft, extravagantly wealthy fellow named Reid Hoffman, who began his fortune with Paypal (boy, what a sorry noxious lot that company has produced!) and then Linkedin. Now, he is shilling an AI play. He advises the rest of us,

> "The answer to our challenges is not to slow down technology, but to accelerate it. Technology is a tool. And the faster we have it in our hands, the better we can solve the problems we have — and the problems it might create."

Phew! The more things change, the more they remain just as fucked-up. As advertised, AI is going to solve everything from climate change to finally finding Santa's workshop at the North Pole. I guess if you made billions of dollars on tech and had to deal with none of the consequences, you'd have unmitigated faith in technology and our technologists have a religious faith in technology's nirvana destiny, as zealous as the most faithful advocates of Buddha, Vishnu, Quetzal-coatl, or the Christ.

Now, there is another view, a view buried by the technologists and their lackeys. It is the understanding gained from looking at the world after two centuries of technological development, that simply stepping on the gas isn't a solution for anything, unless I suppose you're Thelma and Louise, a consciously directed last act, the full embrace of hopeless desperation as freedom. In direct opposition to this thinking is the thought of Werner Heisenberg, who at the age of 23 came up with the revolutionary quantum equations that gave us the bomb and the computer. With "complementarity", Niels Bohr provided Heisenberg's equations with a traditional logic – talk about your philosophy!

As a good German of the era, Heisenberg was deeply classically educated. In a wonderful 1955 book titled *The Physicist's Conception of Nature*, he lays out the historical development of quantum physics from the Greeks to the 17th century scientific revolution that birthed the modern technological world. "Technology is a consequence of science in that a technical exploitation of the forces of nature is generally possible only on the basis of a close understanding of a particular field."

He writes how our human-crafted world differs from the past,

"From the very start we have asked whether the changes in the foundations of modern science might not perhaps be considered as symptoms of shifts in the very basis of our existence, expressing themselves in various places simultaneously, be it in changes of our way of life, in external catastrophes, in wars or revolutions. If, starting from the condition of modern science, we try to find out where the bases have started to shift, we get the impression that it would not be too crude of an oversimplification to say that *for the first time in the course of history modern man on this earth confronts himself alone.*"

Adding,

"The phrase: 'Modern man confronts himself alone' is assuming an ever greater validity in this age of technology. In previous times man felt that he confronted nature alone. Nature populated by creatures of all kinds was a domain existing according to its own laws, to which he had somehow to adapt himself. In our age, however, we live in a world which man has changed so completely that in every sphere—whether we deal with the tools of daily life, whether we eat food which has been prepared by machines, or whether we travel in a countryside radically changed by man—we are always meeting man-made creations, so that in a sense we meet only ourselves."

Most importantly, in direct contrast to our billionaire tech evangelists, Heisenberg notes of our prominently technologically defined era, "Here, extensions of technology need not longer lead to progress." Progress was the slogan of industrialism and now computing. It promotes uncritical development of any and all technologies, ignoring their impact on both the larger society and the greater environment.

Heisenberg defines the situation more complexly, the inherent paradox, the complementary aspects ingrained in all tech development. A simple Bohrian understanding looking at any object from one perspective never provides a whole picture. He offers an alternative way to think than the predominant simplistic tech boosterism:

"Hopes that the extension of man's material and spiritual powers would always spell progress are limited by this situation, if at first somewhat vaguely, the dangers increase as the optimistic wave of faith in progress dashes against this limitation. Perhaps we might illustrate this kind of danger by means of an analogy."

"In what appears to be its unlimited development of material powers, humanity finds itself in the position of a captain whose ship has been built so strongly of steel and iron that the magnetic needle of its compass no longer responds to anything but the iron structures of the ship; it no longer points north. The ship can no longer be steered to reach any goal, but will go around in circles, a victim of wind and currents. However, the danger persists only so long as the captain has not grasped that the compass is not responding to the magnetic forces of the the earth. The moment he realizes that the danger is as good as half-removed; the captain who does not wish to sail in circles but wishes to reach a known or even unknown goal will find ways and means of determining the direction of his ship. He may use a modern compass which is not affected by the iron of the ship, or, as in the olden times, he may use the stars as his guides. Of course, he cannot order the stars to be visible at all times, and perhaps it is true that in our age only a few of them seem to be shining at all, but this one things is clear: the very realization that faith in progress must have a limitation involves the wish to cease going in circles and to reach a goal instead."

An apt analogy for what would become the next 75 year development of the computer industry and the previously established Industrial Era. Our computer technologists encased inside the processor mistake it for a compass, with the larger world either ignored or looked at as just something to be manipulated. Unfortunately 75 years out, our tech captains haven't a clue they have no compass, this limitation, instead they call for, with mixed metaphor apologies, "the pedal to the metal," a crew of Thelmas and Louises with no understanding of what lies just over the horizon they're accelerating into.

Heisenberg suggests two solutions. First, simply understand no one knows where we're going and the continual creation of technology in response to technology provides no direction. Defining technological progress in a world already defined by technology is circular motion, it is no progress at all. "As we become clearer about this limitation, the limitation itself might be considered to be the first foothold from which we may re-orientate ourselves."

Secondly, Heisenberg suggests we must develop technology in relation to the greater world, the universe, not just ourselves. This includes an understanding of the past, the stars of "olden times", though dimmed and some even lost can still help provide direction. An understanding of history, both humanity's own and the earth's natural history can help define goals, not just an endless circling of direction-less technological development determined by the technology itself.

Heisenberg concludes,

"Perhaps this analogy will help us in gaining a new hope that although these limitations affect us in some ways, they do not limit life itself. The space in which man develops as a spiritual being has more dimensions than the single one which it has occupied during the last centuries. This would imply that over longer periods of time, a conscious acceptance of this limitation might well lead to some equilibrium, where man's knowledge and creative forces will once again find themselves ranged spon-taneously about their common centre."

A center that is not technology, but humanity, and as the Ancient Greek Aristotle long ago discerned, *Homo sapiens* is by nature a political animal, yet today our politics are broken. Creating a politics of tech-nology will help revive and reform a healthy, vital politics, a politics necessary to help provide direction to technological development beyond the technology itself.

Today, we are further away from any such politics than we were thirty years ago or 75 years ago at the beginning of the Computer Age. Despite all the promotions of technologists, especially those assuring the empowering of the individual, the one political certainty, the one thing definitively proved over the last three-quarters of a century, the development of AI determined by the technology alone will lead to a greater concentration of wealth and power.

GOD, SCIENCE, AND TECHNOLOGY

There's a long running debate about god and science. A number of advocates over the last couple centuries claim science has buried god, however even a cursory look reveals this hardly to be the case. The first question one is forced to ask is whose god or which god, immediately conjuring all sorts of questions neither helpful or enlightening. Leaving those questions aside, it is without question knowledge gained through science has run roughshod over myths of all religions.

Reading Voltaire, he spends a great deal of time dismissing Judaeo-Christianity because science made obvious many biblical stories were incredulous. In many ways Voltaire had it backwards. Truly, the same thought that created religion was very much the thought that created science. Both stem from the human mind's struggle to understand the world and the universe we find ourselves existing. The thinking underlying all earthly religions is very much the process that gave us science. All religions sought to provide reason behind the seeming chaos of events surrounding, influencing, and impacting human life.

With religion, *Homo sapiens* developed the idea of causality, that every action is preceded by a previous action then followed by another. With this understanding, came the idea events were determined. The forces of nature, indeed our own actions, were determined by greater forces. Today, it doesn't require delving too deeply into science to see these ideas, first created with religion, still lurking and very much alive, most vividly and importantly exemplified by the idea of determinism.

Causal relations are at the root of all science, where any event has been preceded by actions determining whatever follows. This determinism remains the foundation of all science. In many respects, scientific determinism became a new theology. There is a belief, certainly among many physicists and shared by many others, that from the first atom splitting, the universe was set on an inevitable course determined to the end of time. Eddy Keming Chen, a "philosopher of physics" (Richard Feynman violently spins in his grave) at the University of California, San Diego, sums up deterministic belief in a piece in the eminent science journal *Nature*,

> "Take Isaac Newton's laws of motion. If someone knew the present positions and momenta of all particles, they could in theory use Newton's laws to deduce all facts about the Universe, past and future. It's only a lack of knowledge (or computational power) that prevents scientists from doing so."

Newton was a rabidly fervent christian to the point he'd make a fundamentalist in the backwoods of Alabama, I suppose that's a bit of a stereotype, probably better to say in the Halls of Congress, blush. His belief in an ancient deterministic god was essential to shaping his deterministic laws of nature. Four centuries later, Professor Chen brings Newton's determinism to the most bleeding edge of human technology development, compute technology. Underneath the development of much compute technology is a fundamentally deterministic faith, a belief that only the lack of compute power and insufficient data are missing to predict an already determined future. Today, on a daily basis, technology creates ever greater myths and seemingly inevitable fantastical futures. God dead? Not by any means in the Tech Industry. Ironically, 20th century physics, specifically quantum mechanics, in part responsible for the very creation of the Tech Industry, challenged the idea of determinism, replacing the certainty of one action determining the next with probability.

Albert Einstein, one of the founders of this physics, himself the great reshaper of Newtonian physics, remained until death a determined determinist. He once described his motivation, "What really interests me is whether God had any choice in the creation of the world." He was determined to prove God had no choice.

It's fascinating what an important element of determinist philosophy, not science, was in Einstein's ability to devise relativity. There's an excellent piece written by physics Professor Gerald Holton on the entanglement of Einstein's science and his religious thought.

> "He tried to dissociate himself from organized religious activities and associations, inventing his own form of religiousness, just as he was creating his own physics. ...the meaning of a life of brilliant scientific activity drew on the remnants of his fervent first feelings of youthful religiosity."

As with all religion, Einstein's religiosity was most vigorous in its determinism even though his theories of relativity put a radical new spin on the very idea of perspective. Time and space became relative to an observer's position, the speed of light the only universal constant. Ten years later, with the creation of quantum mechanics,

Einstein never accepted its indeterminate universe. Professor Chen's full article "Does quantum theory imply the entire Universe is preordained?," offers a taste of the intellectual hoops physics has since jumped through in trying to keep determinism with attempts to unify Einstein's general relativity with quantum physics.

As queen of the sciences, physics' quantum indeterminacy was revolutionary, yet, over a half-century before, biology launched a similar revolution. An idea appeared with existential implications for humanity, Darwin's theory of natural selection. Copernicus removed the earth from the center of the universe, Darwin removed *Homo sapiens* from the earth's center. Evolution raised the idea of contingency. The great evolutionary paleontologist Stephen Jay Gould explains contingency as follows,

> "The message of history is the theme of contingency. The world makes sense. It's enormously complex. It's full of random elements. What happens makes sense after it happens, if the density of historical information be great enough. It often isn't. That's just the impoverished nature of the record but that's a problem in all historical reconstruction."

Gould continues explaining the important difference between contingency and determinism, especially in regards to many today advocating a simple need for more powerful compute technology and enough data:

> "If the density of evidence be great enough one can explain what happens. It's not an accident, what happened makes sense, but it's not subsumable and predictable under the laws of nature. It's a complex, unrepeatable, unpredictable set of historical contingencies in what happens at the end is so critically dependent on each of the thousands of antecedent steps each happening as they did. No one of which had to happen that way."

"If you could in fact do the great thought experiment, which unfortunately we can't, of erasing life's tape, running it all back and letting it go again would you get anything on the surface of this planet like what we have? Under the biases (determinism) you would get something very close to it, all this is very predictable. Under contingency, you'd never get anything even close to what we see, but you wouldn't get chaos, you'd get a totally different result. It would be equally explainable. The only problem is that the chance of it including any conscious creature desiring to explain it would be very small indeed."

This is a wonderful, succinct exposition of a terribly important concept. It is antithetical to the popular analogy at the beginning of the Scientific Revolution of the universe as a clock. Set in motion, the clock and all its gears will predictably and infinitely go forward – all order deterministically prescribed. Gould emphasizes contingency is not anti-causality. Looking backwards, every given action results from a specific previous action. However, looking forward, you cannot determine precisely which action will happen, unlike a wound clock, the future cannot be precisely or even at times depending how far forward you go generally determined.

Gould continues about determinism's still dominant mind hold,

"We're trained in this hierarchical status ordering of the sciences to think of subsumption under nature's laws as better, as more elegant, as a deeper kind of explanation and of historical contingency as somehow less preferable and messier. It's not true. Contingency is almost never taught."

"There are realms of historical sciences, cosmology, paleontology, geology, and large parts of evolutionary biology that are sort of downgraded in this status order. We don't learn very much about contingency in science. If you want to study contingency, it's a theme much better exploited by humanists, by film makers, by authors, by novelists than by scientists."

Contingency is part of technology's development, yet this is very little understood and dangerously ignored by technologists, who like to proselytize technological determinism in direct opposition to atomic bomb developer J. Robert Oppenheimer. In a 1958 speech, Oppenheimer talked of the accidental nature of plenty of tech development and of science itself:

> "It is a very accidental thing, and again I would say it must be by historians and not by logicians as to what effect, if any, developments in science have on human life. I mean that not primarily in terms of the mechanical differences, although here to it seems to me there's been some mighty odd accidents. Things could have been done with scientific knowledge which lay fallow for a long time because they didn't have any great sex appeal for the economy or the industry of the time and things get done in a great hurry like making an atomic bomb, almost before you knew how, because they do have a great sex appeal. A good deal could be written about the randomness and lack of logic in the relation between what we learn how to do and what we in fact do do."

Oppenheimer and Gould agree this process isn't best or even at all understood by logicians and engineers, but only through history. "What we learn how to do and what in fact we do do" are both contingent.

A simple example of contingency from the recent past combines science, technology, politics, and the development of the American interstate highway system in 1956 with the passage of the "National System of Interstate and Defense Highways Act." Passage of the law was contingent on the Cold War begun a decade before. The Cold War was contingent on World War II, which was contingent on Adolph Hitler. Hitler's rise to power was contingent on the Treaty of Versailles, contingent on World War I. None of these events were automatically determined, all could have been avoided. After all, the magnificent thinker John Maynard Keynes warned in his prescient *Economic Consequences of the Peace* against the Versailles Treaty – no Versailles, no Hitler. Similarly, over the last half-century, the present shape of every major city and the decline of many small towns across America were both contingent on the building of the interstate highway system.

With historical thinking and political affairs, Tolstoy expressed the importance of contingency in the second epilogue of *War and Peace* (1867). He writes,

"For an order to be certainly executed, it is necessary that a man should order what can be executed. But to know what can and what cannot be executed is impossible, not only in the case of Napoleon's invasion of Russia in which millions participated, but even in the simplest event, for in either case millions of obstacles may arise to prevent its execution. Every order executed is always one of an immense number unexecuted. All the impossible orders inconsistent with the course of events remain unexecuted. Only the possible ones get linked up with a consecutive series of commands corresponding to a series of events, and are executed."

Tolstoy concludes, "However accessible may be the chain of causation of any action, we shall never know the whole chain since it is endless, and so again we never reach absolute inevitability."

Tolstoy argued against the then popular, deterministic, great man school of history. He suggested history was immensely more complex than what most perceive today, such that a 21st century American perceives history at all. "The lesson of contingency is the things that seem utterly unimportant for the moment can be those tiny little changes that send history cascading down different pathways." (Gould)

From a humanist view, a biological perspective, and with the equations of 20th century physics serious obstacles to a strictly deterministic view of life have been raised, fairly conclusive objections. Nonetheless, today, determinism remains strongly advocated, peculiarly and particularly as an exclusive force in the development of technology. It is found in the refrain, "you can't stop it," or more recent advocacy of speeding tech development, dubbed accelerationism, as some sort of panacea to solving the great problems caused by the past's indiscriminate and still unmitigated tech development. Underlying both notions lies the idea tech development is predestined to go somewhere, that indiscriminate, continuous technology development is in itself, just as the gods previously, determinant.

With the addition of information, questions regarding determinism versus contingency gain greater complexity, seemingly answered overwhelmingly in favor of contingency. The great mathematician and scientist Norbert Wiener stated, "Information is neither matter or energy." Using feedback, systems incorporate information that manipulates both energy and matter. Feedback is the most important, least understood, scientific concept of the last two centuries.

South African physicist George Ellis states, "The point of a feedback control system is to make the initial state irrelevant as opposed to classic physics in which the initial state determines outcome." A decade ago, in a wonderful talk given in Krakow, Ellis explains a new order created through feedback. He talks of top-down constrained order as opposed to bottom-up, which until recently in the physics' world would pretty much be heresy. As Ellis explains the top establishes "goals" which in turn constrain the bottom. The "top" in this case is order created through feedback. The bottom then the initial state reshaped and constrained by information fed back. "Details of the microstructure control the macrostructure and the macrostructure returns down controlling the microstructure."

Understanding such systems requires the concept of emergence, simplistically defined as the whole being something greater than the sum of all its parts. A great example of this are the 50 – 100 trillion cells that comprise the human body. Each of these cells can be perceived individually but only truly understood in context of their combinations and interactions. Each cell is defined with the organization of individual organs, innumerable processes, and finally the emergence of the human individual.

Human existence, all life, relies on homeostasis, the equilibrium of complexity gained through feedback. Body temperature, heartbeat, blood pressure are all comprised of countless cells "each governed by implicit goals, embodied in the physical structure of the body." Ellis adds the seminal physiologist Arthur Guyton, whose textbook is still standard issue in medical schools, conceived the human body composed of thousands of such systems.

All biological organisms are information dependent systems. "They all have built in through the adaptive process of evolution and embody images of the environment." (Ellis) This is such a wonderful statement, not well understood by most professing evolution. It is a simple, eminently profound understanding that no organism can be understood outside the context of the greater environment in which it was created. Indeed, that greater environment is incorporated into the organism.

With technology development, adopting understandings of contingency and feedback allow an ability to choose and shape technology, an ability at this point that should be perceived necessity for no other reason than allowing us to survive the technology we've already adopted. Without a better understanding of information and feedback, technology development will become even more exclusively determined by a handful of people and increasingly the technology itself. The idea of tech development determined simply by tech development needs to be vigorously opposed. It is the ultimate ignorance of understanding how we've come to be who we are.

In *Nature and the Greeks,* quantum physicist Erwin Schrodinger sought to reveal "what I deem to be the peculiar fundamental features of the present-day scientific world-picture. To prove that these features are historically produced by tracing them back to the earliest stage of Western philosophic thought." It is not simply science that has been historically produced, but politics — the social, cultural, and government institutions surrounding us. Each contain fundamental ideas of determinism as harmful to shaping the future of humanity as tech determinism.

Reforming all these processes needs understanding information and feedback, and a resulting reorganization of institutions and processes. Information and feedback have not just essentially shaped human history, but the history of life. Whatever technology we create, that history will always very much be part of life, ours and all that created us.

NATURAL HISTORY: *OTHERLANDS*

Thomas Halliday's *Otherlands* is a valuable history book. It's a history of earth stretching back 550 million years composed of chapters of a variety of geologic periods and the life forms existing in each time. It's a book that would be more invaluable as a series of images. To his credit, he includes maps of each era, unfortunately the value of including maps is something lost to the book business these days.

History provides context for how and where we've come to be. Much of the time, it is the only context. Too often in the past, knowledge of history was used as a straight jacket in shaping human affairs, instead it should be approached as a vital key to freedom. In regards to freedom, after two centuries of industrial technology, historical perspective is more important today than at any time in the past. The implementation of any technology always destroys part of the past, industrial technology has steam-rolled the past, constructing a present wrongly considered to be severed from all historical roots. Nothing could be further from the truth. Knowledge of the past allows pre-industrial perspectives, perspectives that can help create more varied and vibrant futures.

In a great chapter on the 300 million year ago Carboniferous Period, Halliday directly ties the Industrial Era of the last two centuries to earth's deep past. During the Carboniferous, over the course of tens of millions of years, the earth's vast coal beds were created. At this time, much of earth's land masses were hotter and wetter. "The equatorial sun of Carboniferous Illinois is blinding and white." Plant life exploded. Halliday describes the tree-like *Lepidodendron,*

> "Standing close-knit in the peaty mire is a large patch of trees, each no more than a couple meters from its nearest neighbors and relatively uniform 10 meters tall. Their trunks are crocodile-green, and textured with diamonds overlapping like scales. ...from halfway up each tree to its top, each scale lends support to a single long, thin leaf, a dark brushy bristle, which intermeshes with its closest neighbor.... The light that shines

through the sparse canopy can still be brought to use; in the scale tree, *Lepidodendron,* every part of its diamond-patterned side remains photosynthetic, the whole of the bark able to turn air and sunshine into new plant material."

It is difficult to imagine the energy stored in coal, oil, and natural gas is all derived from ancient sunlight. Photosynthesis, the great energy process of life, takes carbon dioxide from the atmosphere, water from the ground, and light from the sun creating chemical energy for the plant. Oxygen is the byproduct released. Carbon from the atmosphere becomes the plant's main building material. Few understand plants are overwhelmingly creations of the atmosphere, roots providing only stability, water, and a few minerals from the soil. In burning plants or their fossil fuel remains, carbon is released back into the atmosphere, the fire itself a release of the stored sunlight.

Halliday writes of Carboniferous' abundance of carbon, water, and sun:

"With the development of the first tall, tree-like plants – *Calamites,* scale trees, and the conifer-like codaites – all of these ingredients are at their greatest abundance during the Carboniferous. Never before has so much material been concentrated in plants."

Over tens of millions of years, the remnants of this great mass of plants become the coal beds used to fire industrialization three-hundred million years later. The processes that defined human life over the last two and half-centuries resulted only from processes occurring three-hundred million years ago. Halliday writes,

"The irony is that, because of the coal laid down throughout the Central Pangaean Mountains, these places – Illinois and Kentucky, Wales and the West Midlands in Britain, Westphalia in Germany will play a critical role in the earliest rapid industrialization of the eighteenth and nineteenth centuries – the driving force behind the re-release of carbon stored beneath the earth for the last 309 million years. Some 90 percent of all coal on the earth today was deposited during the Carboniferous. It is the sheer abundance of coal, where it was laid down that made it such a cheap, high-energy fuel choice for industrialization, powering steam engines and becoming part of high-quality steel. The legacy of the scale trees lives on."

Little of the history of industrialization properly regards the development of the first great industrial powers was contingent on a process three-hundred million years ago. Nor, that it was a simple matter of happenstance that industrial US, Britain, and Germany advantageously sat atop these coal beds. This fundamental element of industrialization, its deep history, has mostly been ignored. It has been brought to attention only with the larger environmental feedback caused from industrialization's mass burning of fossil fuels.

In burning coal, oil, and natural gas, the energy entrapped, ancient sun energy, is released for work, whether for pushing four thousand pound cars, forging steel, spinning rotors to generate electricity, or radically altering existing ecological systems. Plants are largely products of the atmosphere, upon burning, re-release carbon into the atmosphere, changing the atmosphere's chemical content and altering whatever processes are dependent on the atmosphere, for example climate.

The riot of plant life that occurred in the Carboniferous was contingent on the carbon in the atmosphere – "a number ten times higher than the total amount of carbon dioxide in the atmosphere today." Yet, "compared with the beginning of the Devonian 110 million years before the Carboniferous, the concentration of carbon dioxide in the atmosphere had fallen." After tens of millions of years of plant proliferation, the carbon in the atmosphere had drastically decreased to the point Hadley writes,

"Innovators like the scale trees are radically changing the composition of the atmosphere. The Earth is spiraling towards climate change that will lead to a cooling almost to the point of a global ice age, an increase in seasonality and in aridity, and, ultimately, the wholesale destruction of the very ecosystem that keeps the scale trees alive. This will be their extinction, as the sodden coal swamps of the Carboniferous give way to the drought of the Permian. By removing carbon in such quantities from the atmosphere, they set the stage on which evolution would play out for the next third of a billion years."

I love he uses "innovators," a term in our era of almost godlike veneration. Innovation without context is to say the least problematic. Innovation ignoring feedback is the definition of stupidity. Context can be provided in many different forms, cultural, political, historical, environmental (which in many respects, for example all evolution, is a type of history), and technological. Industrial innovation has largely been valued with limited context and increasingly context is provided exclusively by existing technologies. Industrial technologies have so reshaped human society and the larger environment that certain technologies are perceived as necessity, future innovation constricted by their very existence, certainly no greater example is the United States and the automobile.

Just as importantly, we have ignored the feedback returned from technology's implementation, whether this feedback is social or environmental. We have ignored the fact technology does not in any way remove us from the greater established systems of this small planet. That tweaking one aspect of any system, always results in a reaction creating a new system. Our very definition of intelligence is the ability of a system to incorporate feedback from actions already taken to influence any future actions, with technological development we not simply fail, but flaunt the very notion.

History provides context for the present. In tech defined culture, history is buried, deemed irrelevant, yesterday is forgotten instantaneously. Yet, the whole of industrialization and modernity were defined by a literal digging up of the past. A past now resurrected into the atmosphere. This was done out of ignorance, in the name of innovation. An incapacity to incorporate the feedback of these and many other of our industrial technological actions reveals not a lack of information, but a systemic, or maybe better, a species lack of intelligence. The ability to create species wide intelligence is politics.

SAND COUNTY ALMANAC

Aldo Leopold was one of the first ecologists. Environment and ecology are terms used synonymously, however environment is a more encompassing term, dealing with all physical aspects of any given surrounding. Ecology defines the systemic interactions of biological organisms within a larger environment. Characteristics of any ecological system are very much defined by the greater environment in which it is found. For example, the ecology of a mountain meadow is in part defined by the greater environment of the mountain, such as the altitude, just as the teeming life of a tropical forest is shaped by sun and rain.

Biology, the study of life, is a relatively new science, especially in relation to physics. Certain understandings of biology have been around for thousands of years, but physics as a recognized school of thought and a societal shaping force has had much greater impact over the last five centuries. Such influence by biological science is not much older than a century.

Detrimentally, biology is still too often defined by the conventions of physics, distorting the understanding available with our growing knowledge of ecologies. Physics endlessly divides, seeking fundamental particles and their motion to define everything on top. In certain very important ways, ecological understanding is just the opposite. Any single organism cannot truly be understood without understanding how it interacts with the greater ecological system within which it evolved. Reductionist and determinist analysis, physics, is still very common in looking at ecological systems, yet such thinking alone fails in understanding that knowing any given organism must take into account the greater ecological system by which it was formed.

In 1949, Leopold was one of the first to put forth ecological thinking with his wonderful book, *A Sand County Almanac*. He had spent a lifetime working for the US Forest Service, learning the intricacies of forests and other ecological systems. The book is an essential look not from a physics' perspective of deterministic particles, but a look at whole systems – the perpetual interactions of countless multitudes of individual organisms creating a larger ecological system, and in return, this greater ecological system's effect on each individual organism.

Leopold offers some excellent ideas for understanding ecology. Tellingly he still uses what was then and very much still the established practice of describing ecological complexity as a pyramid, a practice derived from physics. In a world turned upside down by Darwin, pyramids helped continue the wrong-headed notion of human ecological dominance. Today, it is essential to consider ecological systems as distributed networks, webs without centers. Leopold writes,

> "Man is one of thousands of accretions to the height and complexity of the (ecological) pyramid. Science has given us many doubts, but it has given us at least one certainty: the trend of evolution is to elaborate and diversify the biota (the biota being the entirety of biological organisms)."

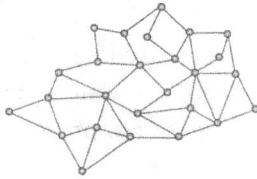

The distributed networked order of ecology

Here, Leopold comments in opposition to the anti-evolutionary results of modern industrial agriculture, which results in the homogenization of ecologies. He then offers a critique of the education system in continuing to limit this understanding, a critique just as relevant today,

> "One of the requisites for an ecological comprehension of land is an understanding of ecology, and this is by no means co-extensive with 'education'; in fact, much higher education

seems deliberately to avoid ecological concepts. An understanding of ecology does not necessarily originate in courses
bearing ecological labels; it is quite as likely to be labeled geography, botany, agronomy, history, or economics. This is as it
should be, but whatever the label, ecological training is scarce."

Leopold is explaining the "division of intellect." While the division
of labor began with the Agrarian revolution 10,000 years ago, the division of intellect became acute with modernity and an ever more
increasingly a barrier to allowing the healthy utilization of the recent
knowledge gained by science and the tsunami of information generated
by our newest technologies.

In the last chapter of the book, "The Land Ethic," Leopold looks at
the practices of industrial farming and its massive impact on established ecologies. He starts with a fundamental insight of the politics of
technology,

"The complexity of co-operative mechanisms has increased
with population density, and with the efficiency of tools. It was
simpler, for example, to define the anti-social uses of sticks and
stones in the days of the mastodons than of bullets and bill-
boards in the age of motors.... Man' s invention of tools has
enabled him to make changes of unprecedented violence, rapid-
ity, and scope."

In looking at *Homo sapiens* historical relation to the land, Leopold
writes,

"There is as yet no ethic dealing with man's relation to land and
to the animals and plants which grow upon it. Land, like
Odysseus' slave-girls, is still property. The land-relation is still
strictly economic, entailing privileges but not obligations."

Just as humankind ethically evolved – with a long way to go – our
relations to each other, for example, slavery is no longer acceptable, we

need to develop an ethic for our relations to the land and its ecologies. Such an ethic is "an evolutionary possibility and an ecological necessity."

He continues,

"All ethics so far evolved rest upon a single premise that the individual is a member of a community of interdependent parts. His instincts prompt him to compete for his place in that community, but his ethics prompt him also to co-operate (perhaps in order that there may be a place to compete for). The land ethic simply enlarges the boundaries of the community to include soils, waters, plants, and animals, or collectively: the land."

"...In short, a land ethic changes the role of *Homo sapiens* from conqueror of the land community to plain member and citizen of it. It implies respect for his fellow-members, and also respect for the community as such."

Leopold critiques the conservation politics his era, which unfortunately can still describe most of today's,

"Despite nearly a century of propaganda, conservation still proceeds at a snail's pace; progress still consists largely of letterhead pieties and convention oratory. On the back forty we still slip two steps backward for each forward stride. The usual answer to this dilemma is 'more conservation education.'"

He adds a completely accurate knock on all environmental and really all present politics,

"The usual answer to this dilemma is 'more conservation education.' No one will debate this, but is it certain that only the volume of education needs stepping up? Is something lacking in the content as well? It is difficult to give a fair summary of its content in brief form, but, as I understand it, the content is substantially this: obey the law, vote right, join some organizations, and practice what conservation is profitable on your own land; the government will do the rest. Is not this formula too easy to accomplish anything worth-while? It defines no right or wrong, assigns no obligation, calls for no sacrifice, implies no change in the current philosophy of values. In respect of land use, it urges only enlightened self-interest. Just how far will such education take us?"

He then rightly concludes,

"To sum up: a system of conservation based solely on economic self-interest is hopelessly lopsided. It tends to ignore, and thus eventually to eliminate, many elements in the land community that lack commercial value, but that are (as far as we know) essential to its healthy functioning. It assumes, falsely, I think, that the economic parts of the biotic clock will function without the uneconomic parts. It tends to relegate to government many functions eventually too large, too complex, or too widely dispersed to be performed by government."

In opposition he writes,

"A land ethic, then, reflects the existence of an ecological conscience, and this in turn reflects a conviction of individual responsibility for the health of the land. Health is the capacity of the land for self-renewal. Conservation is our effort to understand and preserve this capacity."

To creating such an ethic, Leopold hits directly at the greatest established impediment, established economics, which can be considered similar to the values held by the slave-holders of the past and their inability to rid themselves of that "peculiar institution." He writes,

"It of course goes without saying that economic feasibility limits the tether of what can or cannot be done for land. It always has and it always will. The fallacy the economic determinists have tied around our collective neck, and which we now need to cast off, is the belief that economics determines all land use. This is simply not true. An innumerable host of actions and attitudes, comprising perhaps the bulk of all land relations, is determined by the land-users' tastes and predilections, rather than by his purse. The bulk of all land relations hinges on investments of time, forethought, skill, and faith rather than on investments of cash. As a land-user thinketh, so is he."

This is not a fallacy economic determinism has tied around the necks of land use alone, but society as a whole. Leopold adds,

"...to release the evolutionary process for an ethic is simply this: quit thinking about decent land-use as solely an economic problem. Examine each question in terms of what is ethically and esthetically right, as well as what is economically expedient. A thing is right when it tends to preserve the integrity, stability, and beauty of the biotic community."

These last two ideas are essential to developing not only a land ethic, but also a politics of technology. We need to supplant money as the dominant information and communication medium of human social ecology. This need arises not just from the last decades' critical devaluing of money as any valuable information medium, but the essential need to transcend money's long established limitations.

Leopold states "the bulk of all land relations hinges on investments of time, forethought, skill and faith rather than on investments of cash," thus arises the need for information media measuring such values without having to first transform them into crude money relations, that are increasingly controlled by fewer, more clueless, entrenched interests. More complex valuing systems require more than new technologies, but establishing new and maybe reestablishing some old human associations, organizations, and communication processes, particularly in regards to measuring ethical and esthetic worth.

In turn, developing a land ethic requires new ethics for dealing with each other. In the most fundamental understanding of ecology, the parts help define the whole, while the whole in return helps shape each part.

ACKNOWLEDGMENTS

I would very much like to thank Nicco Mele for his vital work putting this book together and Mark Ames for editing assistance on the main essay. A further list of helpful people is far too long, just know, in the words of Ulysses, "I am part of all that I have met."

ABOUT THE AUTHOR

Joseph Costello has spent more than four decades at the crossroads of politics, communications, economics, and energy—fields where power is contested and reshaped every day. He began his career on campaigns from city council races to the presidential level, including serving as Communications Director for Jerry Brown's 1992 presidential run, where he helped redefine political messaging and fundraising. He later advised Governor Howard Dean's groundbreaking 2004 campaign, bringing digital tools into American politics at scale.

Beyond electoral politics, Costello has organized coalitions of energy companies and environmental groups to advance renewable energy in California, helping the City of Santa Monica's electricity supply to be the first in the US to be 100% powered by renewable generation. He worked with Mitchell Kapor and others on the politics of the internet. He represented Mikhail Gorbachev's environmental NGO at the 2002 United Nations Summit on Sustainability in Johannesburg, South Africa. He worked on three presidential campaigns in Africa, two in Nigeria and one in Tanzania.

Drawing on this lifetime of experience, Costello wrote *The Politics of Ape and Machine* to explore how political and economic systems succeed, fail, and can ultimately be reformed through both individual will and collective action. He has written two previous books: *Of By For: The New Politics of Money, Debt, and Democracy* (2012) and *The Politics of Technology* (2016).

BIBLIOGRAPHY

Arendt, Hannah, *On Revolution*, 1963

Arendt, Hannah, *The Human Condition*, 1956

Aeschylus, *Agamemnon*

Aeschylus, *Prometheus Bound*

Aeschylus, *The Eumenides*

Aeschylus, *The Libation Bearers*

Aristotle, *Politics*

Brandeis, Louis, *The Papers of Louis Brandeis*, National Archives

Braudel, Fernand, *The Mediterranean and the Mediterranean World in the Age of Philip II*, 1949

Conrad, Joseph, *Heart of Darkness*, 1899

De Tocqueville, Alexis, *Ancien Régime et la Révolution*, 1856

De Tocqueville, Alexis, *Democracy in America*, 1835

Ellis, George, *On the Nature of Causality in Complex Systems* – Krakow Lecture, 2012

Ferrero, Guglielmo, *The Greatness and Decline of Rome*, 1907

Geoghegan, Thomas, *The History of Democracy Has Yet to Be Written: How We Have to Learn to Govern All Over Again*, 2021

Godfrey-Smith, Peter, *Metazoa: Animal Life and the Birth of the Mind*, 2020

Goodwyn, Lawrence, *Democratic Promise*, 1976

Gould, Stephen Jay, *Tanner Lectures*, 1989

Heisenberg, Werner, *The Physicist's Conception of Nature*, 1955

Huxley, Aldous, *Science, Liberty, and Peace*, 1950

Illich, Ivan, *Tools for Conviviality*, 1970

Jefferson, Thomas, *Letters, National Archives*

Keynes, John Maynard, *Economic Consequences of the Peace*, 1919

Leopold, Aldo, *Sand County Almanac*, 1949

Levine, Yasha, *Surveillance Valley: The Secret Military History of the Internet*, 2018

Lucretius, *De Rerum Natura*

McLuhan, Marshall, *The Gutenberg Galaxy*, 1962

Mcluhan, Marshall, *The Mechanical Bride: Folklore of Industrial Man*, 1951

McLuhan, Marshall, *Understanding Media: The Extensions of Man*, 1964

Mitchell, Thomas, *Athens: A History of the World's First Democracy*, 2019

Mommsen, Theodor, *The History of Rome*, 1854

Nietzsche, Friedrich, *Daybreak*, 1881

Nietzsche, Friedrich, *The Birth of Tragedy*, 1872

Ober, Josiah, *Rise and Fall of Classical Greece*, 2015

Oppenheimer, Robert, *Analogy in Science,* Speech, 1955

Oppenheimer, Robert J., *Princeton University Speech*, 1958

Hallidays, Thomas, *Otherlands: A Journey Through Earth's Extinct Worlds*, 2022

BIBLIOGRAPHY

Payne, Charles, *I've Got the Light of Freedom: The Organizing Tradition and the Mississippi Freedom Struggle*, 1995

Rovelli, Carlo, *Anaximander and the Birth of Science*, 2016

Sapolsky, Robert, *Behave: The Biology of Humans at our Best and Worst*, 2017

Sapolsky, Robert, *A Primate's Memoir: A Neuroscientist's Unconventional Life Among the Baboons*, 2001

Scharf, Caleb, *The Ascent of Information: Books, Bits, Genes, Machines, and Life's Unending Algorithm*, 2021

Schrodinger, Erwin, *Science and Humanism*, 1951

Schrodinger, Erwin, *Nature and the Greeks*, 1954

Shannon, Claude, *The Mathematical Theory of Communication*, 1948

Sheldrake, Merlin, *How Fungi Make Our Worlds, Change Our Minds and Shape Our Future*, 2020

Smith, Adam, *An Inquiry into the Nature and Causes of the Wealth of Nations*, 1776

Szilard, Leo, *On the Reduction of Entropy in a Thermodynamic System by the Introduction of Intelligent Beings*, 1929

Thucydides, *History of the Pelopensian War*

Tolstoy, Leo, *War and Peace*, 1867

Veblen, Thorstein, *The Place of Science in Modern Civilization*, 1919

Warhol, Andy, *The Andy Warhol Diaries*, 1989

Wiener, Norbert, *Cybernetics: Or Control and Communication in the Animal*, 1948

Wiener, Norbert, *The Human Use of Human Beings*, 1950

Wohlleben, Peter, *The Secret Network of Nature*, 2022

Wulf, Andrea, *The Invention of Nature: Alexander von Humboldt's New World*, 2015

Zaitchik, Alexander, *Owning the Sun: A People's History of Monopoly Medicine from Aspirin to Covid-19 Vaccines*, 2022

INDEX

www.ingramcontent.com/pod-product-compliance
Lightning Source LLC
Chambersburg PA
CBHW070907270326
41927CB00011B/2490